THANK
EARTH
YOU

Published by Armand Daigle

Copyright © 2014 by Armand Daigle
www.drenchedinelectricity.com

Edited by David Kassin Fried
www.dkfwriting.com

Design by Armand Daigle

ISBN: 0-991-3108-0-2

Author photographs © Erin Molloy Photography

All names have been changed or omitted to protect the identities of those
involved.

THANK

EARTH

YOU

BY

ARMAND DAIGLE

My Sweet and Pure Marie,

Your never-ending & continuous positivity
& joy for... pretty much everything... inspires me
more & more each day. I hope to learn even
just a sliver of how you do it. You treat me
so well. I am galactically grateful for you.

With TLC,

Armand

Everything in this book has always been here.

Thank you, Ava—for reading this even though you hate to read.

May we stand together at the maelstrom

.

CONTENTS

PART I: BELLWETHERS

SAUSAGE PRESSURE

I'm sitting in an examination room, waiting for a man semi-famous around town for his vasectomy procedures. Lining the wall across from me are pictures of men in hip yet nondescript shirts and jeans, wearing big, fake smiles while they high-five their doctors. To the right, there's a strange, subtly angled operating table with a short, grooved seat slid up tight beside it that looks like a device saved for specialized cases or when someone's got something notches above bad.

For six months, the pain has been mild; manageable would be a good description. It's not enough to make my parents privy, but they aren't about much in my life these days. I've also been putting this visit off for so long—busy with work, "I'll go after my next deadline"—that I don't really remember what it's like to have normal testicles. Would the discomfort be more noticeable if I had a different job? Would the procrastination subside? Even now while I'm somewhat nervous about what the doctor might find, mostly I'm thinking about how late I'll have to be at the office tonight to catch up on the hours I've missed.

The constant worry, the hard-to-reach subcontractors not making schedule, the early morning *oh shit* e-mails, the unnecessary budget-eating meetings, the over and over and over—it's all wrapped up into a big, fat bee that dwarfs the physical pain and buzzes around in my head, with unlimited stingers and tiny, mocking laughs. Things go so fast during the day that she's kept quiet at work, but she enjoys cranking up the volume after hours until I can't hear anything else, forcing me to spend a quarter of my money on booze and Oreos just to shut her up and relax.

And so she goes.

The door clicks open and I get a first look at Dr. Slice, the man whose name years ago I saw on salvaged shirts with the various and obligatory plays on words. He's much older than I'd expected but grips my hand like a vise. After he introduces himself, I look to the floor—a crutch I've unconsciously developed over the long haul—and almost get through giving him my name before he says, "So, what can I help you with?"

I'm sorry, Doctor. The middle of my sentence interrupted the start of yours. Forgive me.

"Well, it's not really pain, more like an uncomfortable feeling that I've had in my testicles for a couple months," I say, understating the duration. "I've gone to two other doctors, went through all their tests, but neither could tell me what's wrong."

"Describe the pain for me."

"It's not terrible. It's as if someone were grabbing, maybe gently squeezing them . . . but at all times."

"Well, let's take a look."

Dr. Slice scoots his stool toward me like he's on his way to some chore, and then his eyes look into mine as if he knows something I don't, something that's just innocent enough for him to give me a wink.

Don't. Just . . . don't wink at me right now. Thanks.

I slide my khakis and boxers to the ankles, and Dr. Slice begins to test my instrument. While he's getting comfortable at crotch level, I tell him the discomfort came after a weekend at a friend's lake house where I wore a life jacket like a diaper for most of two consecutive days. I don't tell him of the prolonged nut hugging, but I do say, "perhaps there was some bacteria in the water that swam up the urethra?"

"Pfff. That's not it." I imagine him thinking he can't wait to get off work so he can go home and polish the medical awards above his staircase.

"Hmm. Okay. Take your boxers all the way off and put your elbows on the table."

Um . . . elbows?

One after another, arm hairs stand up, but I do what I'm told. I'm half naked and moving to where he wants me when the short seat stops my knees from bending as I awkwardly try to lean over the table; motor reflexes take over and my right leg lifts, allowing the knee to slide perfectly into one of the two grooves. The same thing happens with my left leg, and everything clicks at once. The seat below me isn't a seat at all; it's a knee rest designed to properly elevate the body.

Dr. Slice makes a noise over my shoulder. I gulp hard.

"Relax," he says, now directly behind me. "Take a nice, deep breath."

No. He can't be thinking that. The pain is in my—UH!

AHHHUUUUUHHHAAAHHH!

Dear God! Every thought I have is overpowered by pressure—enormous pressure in a place I've never felt it before. He's only inserted two fingers, but it feels like I'm on a farm and he's elbow deep. His free hand comes around to the front of me to press in on my lower abdomen, issuing an intense ballooning feeling that sends the experience skyrocketing up the pain index. And his breathing next to my ear is even and superior as he works me like a drunk ventriloquist. (None of the awards Dr. Slice hangs above his staircase say the word "gentle.")

Both my body and mind struggle from the severe lack of warning; every muscle is clenched tight, unable to move. And yet he somehow goes in further, to places no one has ever been, where time isn't a concept anymore, where all there's left to cling to are the sharp spasms shooting through my taut skin bag.

Years pass while the massive pain storm rolls in my head, although deep in the intrusion, there are only brief flickers of reality. Wherever I am my brain isn't able to gain control, but luckily instincts don't require much. They tell me I can keep on fighting these violent sausage fingers with all my strength or completely let go and step aside for my puppet master. I can't imagine the latter could feel any worse . . . so I choose surrender.

I'm yours, Dr. Slice. Do as you must. Take me.

My muscles relax one by one. As I let go, pee dribbles on the knee rest and drips down to pool on the floor, but not a cell in my body cares because the pain is diminishing. I let go further, until my entire body goes limp and I become jelly. Slick with armpit sweat, my elbows slide wide on the table.

My head and neck sink between them while my abdomen loosens in odd, discrete steps before filling out to its normal, droopy condition. And with everything else spoken for, all of my sphincters stand down.

The pressure is still savagely measurable, but the shooting pain has left my insides, allowing the examination room to reconstitute. Dr. Slice continues to root around under my hood, and I can't help but wonder if he's painting a mental picture of my insides, amplifying his senses like blind men do, or is he purely focused on the strict mechanics, the methods, the by-the-book of it?

At long last I feel him start to pull out. He eases up on my front, and the industrial grade clamp on my midsection loses its hold. His fingers hesitate at the exit for longer than they should, but thank my lucky chicken he finally gets them out of me and cabin pressure is restored. He backs away in silence, leaving me exhausted and sprawled out over small puddles of my own fluids, thinking, *Until now my mother is the only one who's ever seen me like this.* As I try to catch my loud, uneven breaths, Dr. Slice removes his gloves and sighs with a slight tinge of pleasure. Motor control creeps back, and my legs quake from the virginity he's stolen, but my thoughts are only on the man stepping on my boxers as he crosses the room. How Dr. Slice must look at the world. How he must look at the men of the world. Having the ability to completely change someone's day for good or for bad, having these intimate interactions be a part of his everyday work—I couldn't imagine. Does the power of routine desensitize him to what he's actually doing, and everything else for that matter?

Desensitized or not, he's getting his things together while I still feel like a sex doll, naked and used, having no idea what just happened, what Dr. Slice has given me. I'm sure he has no idea either. I try to read his face, but he makes no attempt to acknowledge his last appointment of the day; he just reaches into a cabinet and tosses a box of Kleenex at me like he's throwing meat scraps to his dog. He makes his way to the exit, but before he leaves, before the steel bolt clicks in the door, this semi-famous, award-winning doctor looks over his shoulder and says:

"I'm done. Clean yourself up."

DEADLINE ANARCHY

The hills grow plush and robust, the blue above them is cloudless, the sun's intensity bathes the land just right, birds serenade their mates in easygoing breeze, and just like every other work day, double-paned glass separates me from it all. The cubical window is a brutal and evil creation, offering nothing but futile hope framed in persistent torture. Inside, I and the other poor souls around me are chained to the promise of our country's tender, the value of which being only what we give it.

Dammit, I need to focus, need to get these last few piping drawings marked up. For weeks, our engineering team has been in a frenzy, copying the work of an overseas firm, just so we can put our Texas stamps on the plans, enabling the facility addition project to go through the permit process. We've stayed up all hours of the night, poring over hundreds and hundreds of drawings, checking the math and building codes, adding a couple lines to each sheet, and replacing their standards and symbols with those of our own. This race called Tedium has come down to the wire, and the architect is on our backs, kicking us mercilessly and yelling, "Faster! Faster!" I'm told of the importance of my job and this project, but I constantly question the value I'm adding.

The buzzing from my phone slides it across my desk, and when I see the face on the incoming call I barrel out of my cubical, past all the new age slaves, to an empty conference room down the hall—the only place in this impenetrable fortress that gets a good signal.

"Hey," Ava says. "I have the best news!"

"You bought me that cheetah-print thong? No wait. Did someone figure out how to make a lava-safe surfboard and you lost the bet?"

"Haha. First of all, you're crazy. Second, shut your lovely mouth. You know that's impossible. No, I found out what those glowing organisms are called! Dinoflagellates."

"Oh, well yeah," I say, acting like I've known all along. "Everybody knows that."

"Yeah, right. Do you think I could perfect their technology and make a dress or skank-skirt that sparkle-glows purples and blues, but only when I'm dancing? Halloween's gettin' close, you know."

I don't know how I would get through my day without this woman.

Outside the conference room, I see my coworker Magnus rush past with rolls of drawings in hand and stop midstride when he catches me out of the corner of his eye. He turns toward me much slower than necessary to stare with his trademark, vacant face.

"Ava. You don't need to perfect their technology. You already have that sparkle-glow on the inside."

Magnus looks left, then right. He unbuttons his shirt.

"Aw. You're too much. Or maybe, just right. What are you doing later? Comedy at my place?"

Magnus takes a highlighter from his pocket, uncaps it, lifts up his undershirt, then runs the tip in circles around his left nipple.

I clear my throat. "Um. Man, that's exactly what I need right now. Not sure if I can, though." Hearing something or someone down the hall, Magnus quickly tucks his shirt back in and jogs away from the window. "We got a big package due on Friday. Might need to stay late this whole week."

"Ah, bummer, dude. Well, let me know. I'll let you get back to it. Love you."

"I love you so much, starshine."

Getting back to my desk, I find my water glass with my cubical nameplate, all my mechanical pencils, and their taken-out-and-broken-up leads soaking inside. Next to it is a Post-it note that reads: ESTEBAN DID IT.

"That's fine," I murmur. "That's just fine."

Magnus is a few cubes down, wearing a shit-eating grin and pretending to work. He looks up at me and I look back, giving him a dose of his vacant face. On the table next to him, I place my arm between the cube wall and his drawings, notes, calculations, binders and sweep it clear across, sending all of his day's work to the floor. Magnus's lips press tight, fighting off any sign of a smirk. I then pick up his recycled drawing bin and empty it all over his desk, never taking my eyes off the smug bastard. "You shouldn't make so many mistakes," I say. "Your recycling bin was getting really full."

Half an hour later, a handful of pennies crashes down on my monitor, keyboard, and arms. My back wrenches from the surprise, and I hear a muffled chuckle a few cubes down.

Just wait. Just you wait.

I rush the drawings over to one of the drafters because I know he's been dragging ass lately. I give him the sheets and find out he's a few hours behind where he should be. I stand there in silence, looking at his screen, and he slowly realizes I'm beyond frustrated. I tell him that we need to pick up the pace a bit or I'll have to stay late to finish his work. And then I walk away with regret and a bad taste in my mouth, because when we're slammed, by late afternoon I can hear myself sounding like my bosses.

As usual, my frustration leads to distraction, and I do an online search for a study my friend told me about the other day. After reading a few articles, I'm taken by the chance that starlight could be all we need in the future. If horizontal gene transfer hits mainstream, we'll have no choice but to add more words to the definition of evolution. Governmental institutions will lose a chunk of their power. And it will all be thanks to the eastern emerald elysia—the sea slug that adopted photosynthesis and evolved to live without food.

One of my bosses rushes into my "office" and tells me we just won a hefty project and got shortlisted for another. He asks me when this current project ends, and it's apparent that we need to set up a team meeting to discuss the reality of major schedule overlap. My Christmas bonus better make up for this workload that's already erased my summer and help pay for my sabbatical with Ava to anywhere but here.

The only good thing about staying late is that I get to work desperately in a quiet setting while rush hour comes and goes.

I plow through the drafter's unfinished work for a couple of hours before the needle on my tank points to empty. Before I leave for the night, I check my personal inbox out of habit and find a string of forwarded emails, each one more frantic than the last. My mother's always up in arms about some political rumor or current event that's spreading like wildfire through the hungry nodes of the Internet. In the last of her emails, she proclaims that she and my dad are getting ready to move to Europe because the siege of anarchy is rolling in. I wish she would try to take a step back, to see the increasing good in this world and not send these emails every month or two.

I'm the only car on the highway heading home, but I get worked up about my mother. My toes are white on the accelerator. My already aching back has gotten tighter. I try to tell myself to calm down, and instead, revel in the global potential of sea slugs.

SPRING CHICKEN

The grip at the glutes and just above the knees, the soft aged denim, are why I usually wear the same jeans on nights like these. Despite the daily creep and growth of the frays and the loss of luster in the indigo dye, I've never found a pair that have fit so natural, so well, so "this makes absolute sense." For different reasons in similar times, Ava is also accustomed to repeat wears of her army-style, drawstring affair. "That's how I know if I'm back or not," she says. "If I look down and the brown and green aren't separated, I'm not back yet."

Ava. Beautiful, zesty, spunky, voluptuous, passionate Ava.

It's icicle weather, and a group of us are holed up in her garage for the evening. My crony Brown Sugar grips Spring Chicken by the fur on his head and the ring above his ankles and stretches him. The rest of us look on as the amber in Ava's eyes gives way to blackness like I've seen so many times before. And all I can do is smile, knowing what comes next.

For as long as I've known her, she's wanted to get into the middle of things: Texas Redbud, homemade discs of fried cheese, music- and love-fueled group hugs, the froth and splash of waterfalls, swales of mud, shirts that others wear, the sizzle-sand curl of waves right before they crash, speaker towers, bubbles taller than men, low mirages in the crown of sun. Ava wakes to permeate through the surfaces, to explore the depths, to squat small among the innards. And in this protocol of pleasure, she wears the brown and green pants while her procedure drips with a sort of sexual metaphor that's seemingly flecked with deviance, yet her wonder holds the only true place here.

"I wanna get up in it," she says, cute but mischievous. "What if I just get up in it a li'l bit?"

Ava views the world as a painter's palette for her to dab her brush across and get the best colors from; she even claims she's had brief terms of tetrachromacy. She's a vintage lemon press with a full clamp on life, and the harder her hold, the more I love her. She turns heads, both because of her zeal and her sultry Mediterranean look, and since we first fixed eyes on each other, she's set my world afire. Living has become something more tangible, something more malleable, as if I've gotten a step closer to paradise.

She was a heavy weight coming off ten consecutive years of relationships when we met and made me out to be a spring chicken—perpetually single aside for a few months. But when we come together now, our sparks flower new species and illuminate cold rocks in the far depths of space. She's become an alluring distraction from my bouts as a drudge and has awoken a drive in me to celebrate the gift of the present—a drive I hope never gets turned off. When she has a dream that raises a question, I have a dream that brings the answer. And over the last year, our approaches and experiences have blended more and more—to the point now where we have become tethered.

Before she gets inside her mark, flirtatious rituals must be gone through, so she walks around with fingers that glide, not committed to touching, only to suspense. She surveys the specimen while stroking imaginary whiskers, then gets closer for the next stage of probing. She sneaks, she smirks, her gears whirr at top speed, and she tries the waters (or mud, or flowers) with a foot, a hand, or a finger. Then, embodying a dart, she plunges herself into lands untouched by animal, where the excitement of the new enhances the throb of her heart. Her body then gushes in giggles, spreading new life to those watching, and it is this passion that takes us by the hand, enabling us to feel and digest as she does. Everyone partakes inside Ava's spellbinding world.

The arousal is reaching advanced levels now, testing our thresholds and cinching our thighs closer together. Because she's about to bring us back there again, as she prepares to deflower a plush and stuffed animal in her garage.

Spring Chicken, a name given by Ava, isn't really a chicken at all, but a duck—a yellow, furry duck—with a huge spring extending from his butt. In full compression, he's only a foot tall and round as a baby, but when you pin his feet down and pull him up, his head can touch the ceiling. He doesn't have any legs per se, just the spring, ankles, and polyester feet . . . and apparently he's a he.

I found him at a thrift store for a dollar and at once envisioned a ridiculous rendezvous with Ava. Since then, he's been to rivers and restaurants, seen a biker rally and quite a few laser dance parties, been hugged by many friends, even strangers, and seen me when I've been at my worst. It's amazing, the gems you find at thrift stores when you're not even looking—antique dreams waiting to be new again. Forgotten chickens wasting away on dusty shelves, hoping for a new owner before the next spring. In a weird twist of fate, and no matter how often I joke about him, Spring Chicken has become one of my muses. And coming along just before him, Ava has too. They remind me that life should be fun, even silly at times. They remind me not to take myself too seriously, that sometimes I just need to chill out, be less controlling, and simply let life happen.

It's potent and midnight as my two muses meet, and in a few minutes, they'll become intimate. This moment will stand the test of time and will help me stand it too.

A frequent, inadvertent low-rider, Ava is sitting on her couch, her army pants stuck in a provocative fall down the supple contours of her pelvis. She raises her bare foot into position, making the pant leg slide down to reveal immaculate, olive skin, while Brown Sugar steadies and extends the rings, the rest of us becoming silent. Her toes linger at the entrance just for a bit, then like a piston she kicks her foot and leg up, up through the rings of Spring Chicken's spring. It doesn't look or feel like any violation, but a welcomed breaching, even a practiced dance. The spring lengthens and intertwines with her leg, giving it a soft, yellow hug, wrapping around her curves in a perfect fit of bundled ecstasy. With each loop her foot passes, each inch the spring slips down her skin, we all feel the growing giddiness, the seduction in our stomachs and on our faces. And the newfound vividness, the same rushing wave of awe shooting through the group makes us wonder whose hair is rubbing on whose. She hits the last of the coil but pushes further, unsatisfied until she delves as deep into the virgin land as she can, until her toes barely touch Spring Chicken's underbelly. She tickles his plush fur with her big toe.

"How does it feel?" we ask like children, almost wetting our pants in excitement.

"That's it," she says. "Yep, that's fine. This is normal. It's fine . . . mmmmm . . . what about this?!" She jabs her foot against Spring Chicken's underside, pressing him with her leg, wiggling her big toe in his nether regions until her foot blends into the fur. "Did you ever think of that?!"

She keeps it up for a few moments, then notices the look in our eyes and realizes what she's doing. She bursts out in laughter, her leg recoiling from the furry spirals, and tries to apologize for her wonderful behavior. "I'm so sorry, everyone! No, no, don't look at it! Hahaha. Don't look at it!"

While Ava tries to rein herself in and regain composure (we all know it'll be hard for her to come back now), I bring the deflowered duck into my clutches to test him out, see how limber he is, how far he can stretch. I use the handle that dangles from a string attached to his head to hook him on the mechanical door track. I then make it some ten or fifteen feet across the garage before I feel the spring begin to give. Underneath his cotton candy fur, I imagine every molecule is being pulled away from its neighbor, the interstitial space growing wider and wider and closer to the brink of irreversible damage. After a few seconds there, I have to let him go, hoping he'll return to his normal self, not wanting him to be a casualty of my temporary abandon. He whizzes past Ava's head, making her highlighted hair dance, and clanks off the garage door back toward me before swaying like an animated pendulum—a dizzy body on his way to homeostasis. His face is still yellow and blank, but I know what's going on inside: he's having a blast, that adorable guy. He's running around in Stuffed Animal Land, quacking, tooting hand horns, and spanking his backside.

When the goofball comes to rest, I hug him, and Ava and I check his exterior for injuries. Everything looks and feels normal, no signs of permanent stretching. We run the rest of the necessary diagnostics, and once we're satisfied, we high-five to Spring Chicken not losing a spring in his step.

I still have him to this day, over three years after his first meeting with Ava. He's actually twenty or so feet from me right now—a yellow, furry muse in the dark of my closet— under boxes of old engineering documents, in a basket sur-rounded by and intertwingled with brilliant blue and neon orange boas, in a cacophony of color and texture that warms my heart.

I've asked myself why this night was so special, why it keeps resurfacing. It's taken me over two years to fully realize the gravity of what went on in Ava's garage. It is, in my mind, what life is all about: these moments that you can go to and live eternally. This is one of the memories I'll think about while sitting at the edge of insanity. In the next few hours, this will be one of the memories that brings me back from death.

PART II: JUPITER MOON FIRE

POWER-UP PELT

The four of us are holding hands in a circle—one hand up, one hand down—seeking to find balance in the fold. After a moment of silence, Antonio says he wants us to speak our intentions and bless the journey we're about to take.

I'm just a pup with these outward engagements, and I have to admit I've been shy to embrace them. The process is a huge departure from my rigid upbringing; it requires a wrench that was never placed in my toolbox. I've also been toiling for so long in the A-through-X columns of project spreadsheets that it's taken a while to shake myself from the grid. But Antonio's light shoulder touches and the way he leans into his conversations relaxes me and reassures that he's here to support me however he can. There's a thickness to him, an inkling that he really wants to listen.

Still, it's hard when you're as fresh out as me. You gotta take the time to get acclimated. During all those long days that ended before they began, there were so many distractions that kept me in my comfy shell, kept me from broadening my reach, or maybe I'm just placing blame because it's always easier to shift responsibility somewhere else. And why not? I have so many culprits to point my finger at: putting up with my job because it pays well and I only hate it every other day, feeling safe in a relationship, unlocking the magic amulet, "next year will be different," the taste of ice cream when I put it in between Oreos, making long digressions, etc. But I'm not thinking about any of this now. It all seems miles away tonight.

Antonio begins with how much he appreciates that we were all able to make this trip—especially since the one-year anniversary falls on a full moon. He offers support for us and believes in our project because "it feels right, and we'll continue to do it as long as it does." Antonio is love's biggest champion and the founder of our production company inspired by wolves, which is why his intention for us to bolster our pack and get some dirt on our backs is more than fitting. He talks in weird ways at times, can wear a mustache better than most, and is a devout lover of dogs. You could also say he's agile and doglike, but above everything he believes in being a good person, which is a big reason why I'm drawn to him and why he's the sexy soul he is.

Across from me is Cyrus. He's a little on the stocky side, and also does well in the hair department. He's a laidback dude with gentle eyes, but when he needs to throw it in gear he can flash a mean, cheek-flexing side bite. His enthusiasm for art is more than impressive, and he speaks of progress for our group. He yearns for our advancement, for us to conquer the mountain we're working to climb. He wants to create art that kicks and backflips and snarls; in other words, he wants the animal in us to come out. But at the heart of it, he's a feral man who loves nothing more than to dance and howl his hide off with his friends.

Taking his baton of betterment, I circle on, imagining each of us as one paw, one leg, all working together to run as one wolf. Since I was a child, I've wrestled with a stutter, but after years of speech therapy I learned to hide it, shaping me into a short, quiet observer. Other than why I don't talk much, I've always been asked what my cultural background is. And though I like to wear bright colors at metal concerts and black at peaceful gatherings, people say I'm reliable. What I'm intent on is finding the new idea, somewhere past the edge of perception where no one's been. I want to catch it and bring it back so we can nurse it, nurture it, and share it with everyone. In my utopia, as the sun comes around in the east, we'll be feverishly building the horizon, laying the foundation brick by brick from just beyond the shadows, where every second our feet narrowly avoid the arms of dawn.

The last but strongest paw, Diego, talks about action. He keeps a tan, slim figure, and often raises his eyebrows when he talks, but whatever he says is usually followed by quick work and etched in gold. He's a concrete man who enjoys doing, getting in the trenches, bringing ideas alive. He wants us to realize, catalyze, and improvise; hopefully, before the night runs out, we'll put a few projects in motion.

What Diego doesn't know is that later in the evening, I'll become a starchild on a planet at the other end of the universe, gazing up at a moon that I don't know the name of. I'm guessing it'll have some sort of letter and number combination like S/2011 P 1. But the point is this: even there, on that remote planet, our pack feels right. We're together—all of us—under one pelt.

So when Antonio wants to climb up the hill on the other side of the creek because he feels like he needs to get closer to the sun, we all want to climb up the hill on the other side of the creek to get closer to the sun. Preparing for the hike, we select our power-ups, drink orange juice, grab some road beers, and go find our walking sticks. With all the necessary preparations complete, our trek begins single-file up toward the wind-chimey, gardeny plot on our side of the creek. The excitement of the soundtrack for this part of the journey—the immaculate pinging and ringing of nature and man shaking hands—is just setting in when Cyrus breaks up the yonder soothing by farting from the back of the line. Methinks he's either nervous or tonight will be getting weirder sooner than I thought. Or both, mayhaps. Probably both. A few moments later, my suspicions are confirmed when a fat burp interrupts my yawn.

As I become immersed in this outdoor world—away from AC, bathrobes, ottomans, and street-side Tuesday garbage pickup—I'm perplexed by the months in advance we needed to plan for a single uninterrupted night in the bosom of our creation. The rawness, the indiscriminate, and grime thrive like weeds out here in the den where we wolves came from, but dammit, this is some good nature. I wish we could put it in to-go containers and take it with us back to our offices or wherever we desire, maybe dipping into it later for a midnight snack. Out here though, nature never clocks in or clocks out. There's no nine-to-five in these parts.

"I'm going to be in this one place for my entire life." That's what the tree says. But think of the timelines she'll see.

Through the years, I've learned that this is why nature rewards patience. You gotta wait for her, and at the right time, she'll turn up the volume. She'll make sure nothing else eclipses you; she'll show you the flower that you really are.

A raised cave comes up on our left. Antonio—channeling his best Ava—wants to explore the innards. He scales the rock façade in no time and peeks inside while Diego takes pictures with an old camera that looks like a cross between an early sci-fi spaceship and one of those fake binocular-flasks. "We can use it as a prop on our next project," Diego says, meaning the camera. I'm glad he's taking pictures now and not later, because if Diego is anything like me, he'll either be getting shots of his shoes for fifteen minutes or forget how to turn it on.

Nights like these I turn into a ninety-five-year-old or a tribesman in the Amazonian jungle who's never seen a cell phone before. We're not that deep yet, though. Right now, I could still operate devices, even ride a bike for a short while. Entering the animal realm is what my old boss used to call it, and while the expression's stuck over the years, tonight I'll discover brand-new meaning in the bizarre and the bubbly. But all that peace and viciousness comes much later, though. Time drags its feet from here on out.

Antonio reports back that the cave is shallower than he once guessed. His head then perks up, like a dog's when he senses someone or something coming.

"We gots to go."

No one questions him, we just nod our heads and follow because something is calling for him, something beyond and above the wind chimes, the waterfalls, the grotto, and the creek beside us—and that's good enough for now.

27

He walks fast, each step more purposeful than the last. We stay in stride as best we can, but we all notice we're a pace or two short of jogging. Antonio pushes harder, and it doesn't take too long until we're four legs of an animal, loping and bounding up the creek, hopping across the half-submerged rocks that may have once been used for skipping by the Tree Giants I'll see later. We pass by two women soaking their feet in the swimming hole down on our left, and I know we're all thinking the same thing: interaction with other people is less than optimal right now. *Other people? Oh no! I'm afraid.* A part of me also can't help but think their feet must be freezing. And another part of me fixates on the awesome reality of that even being an option on the first full moon of the year. I love you, Texas. I love you, mucho.

We keep ascending, rock by rock, guided only by the sun and an inkling, and half-way up the slants, the great assembly of saffron daggers make their stand. It's not that I see them beam off of the rocks, or leaves, or streams, it's that I see the rays themselves. I mean just thick and there. They appear like stoic fire cutting through the clouds and canopy, still fresh from their 92 million-mile journey to see me, as if the sun was saying, *Just reminding you that I can touch anything I want! Anytime, anywhere, I'm always here. I'm always doin' it.*

You do it, Sun. Sunshine, do it!

"You guys feelin' weird yet?" Diego asks.

Cyrus and Antonio mutter responses, but my attention isn't up to par.

I drop my walking stick to the side of the stream beneath us, wanting to be free of such devices, to travel light. *I grow weary of your presence, stick. Go be with your friends.* At this point, whatever I hold I'll probably lose or drop in water anyway.

Too many objects on my person means the subconscious is constantly banging around in my wrinkly piece of head-gum. That constant attention on superfluous items takes away from the focus on what's directly in front of me. (I also prefer little to no condiments on my food, thank you.) Up high on the hill, our ascension is halted by a fence with a red-and-black sign: NO TRESPASSING.

Maybe it's just my heightened sensitivity right now, but the aggression cuts me—a banner flown high and frequent, a remnant of a time of great tumult, anger, fear, and isolation. Though it turns us back for now, our spirit remains steadfast, for there's much to do and we know we'll cross each other's path again soon.

Splendor, Hilarity, and Epiphany will be arriving shortly, so we leap and bound back down to our camp, eager like young pups to see what comes next.

CUBICAL GLITTER

For twenty-eight years I've been quiet, punched a calculator, taken steps my father has wanted me to, studied differentials and equations I've never implemented, obtained a nuclear engineering degree I've never used, and worked on projects that were either carbon copies or doomed from the start. For the last five of those twenty-eight years, I was a mechanical engineer locked in an eight- by eight-foot prison, just another element slowly rotting away fifty hours at a time in the all-too-common cubical array. I've cut the loose threads off my dress pants, helped design process systems in a cutting edge pharmaceutical facility, worked with Fortune 500 companies, trained young engineers, became a project manager, and acquired a professional engineering license.

During the same twenty-eight years, I've built forts big enough for a family; played baseball with more passion than I've given anything else; learned to mute-ride the low E string in metal songs; chugged beers while wakeboarding; experimented with mind alteration and mind expansion; grown my hair out; gone to raves; worn cheetah-print thongs and jeans with more holes than Mom would ever like to see; cut video compilations of boat parties with my belligerent friends; had altitude sickness cured at Machu Picchu; played with Ava in volcanic lava; resonated with Joseph Campbell and Terence McKenna; seen Alex Grey paint live; and been lucky enough to go to the Coachella Valley Music and Arts Festival for a second time.

A few months after my twenty-eighth birthday, Spring Chicken and I came to a dichotomous tipping point, where day and night took swords to each other.

It's 12:37 a.m. I'm sitting on an actress's kitchen floor, somewhere between 4th of July fireworks and swamp ass, while beautiful, red, fleshy hills roll past me in the night. Starting and ending at infinity, hand clasps hand over and over—the fingers nestled between each other—forming the velvety slopes, sweeping and streaking the backs of my eyelids.

It's 6:00 a.m. My heart races from my blaring alarm.

"Holy shit. . . . Ugh."

Gotta turn that down. But must brush teeth fast now. Shower. Make it to work so there's enough time to research diaphragm valves before eight o'clock conference call. Missed call from Mom. Dammit. Still haven't gotten back to her. Seem to be forgetting the simplest tasks.

It's 12:45 a.m. Magnus and I are talking about redshifting, what happens at the "ends" of the universe, and what if the culmination of life is for all humans to transcend to the next level of consciousness, but that next level is just a room at the end of the wormholes where we have to find a hiding spot and wait for our guest of honor, Tony Danza, to arrive, and yell "Surprise!" at just the right moment? And then blackness. Nothingness.

It's 6:45 a.m. I'm halfway to work, taking my eyes off the road for the full moon while listening to a French, electronic rock duo and thinking up a music video featuring creatures with squid-like appendages frolicking on the horizon of some surreal landscape. At the climax of the song they erupt in an orgy of celebration, cast in red shadows on the early morning sky. Anything to take my mind off a conference call where I'm going to get bitched at by clients because my solution is going to cost them too much money, even though they've had this information for months.

It's 10:14 a.m. My boss just walked into my cube, asking to see notes from a construction site visit I went on last week. I look through all the charts, project proposals, calculations, and drawings, not finding my notes.

"Sorry. I'm not seeing it. Let me check my backpack."

My boss waits while I go for the backpack zipper that's not too many more uses away from being completely worthless. I check the papers in the first compartment, but it's all just concert ticket print-outs, engineering handbooks, and empty packages for LED lights. I'm unzipping the next compartment when something happens on the floor beside my backpack.

Oh no.

I angle the backpack up fast and move it to cover the gold-and-magenta glitter that's spilled out into a semi-circle on my cubical floor. I look up quick to my boss, trying to hide my embarrassment. Lucky for me, my boss's impatience took over and he's been checking his phone because even he's being smothered by the wet blanket of deadlines today. (At the peaks, even the nicest of my coworkers get frustrated if they have to wait more than a few seconds.)

"I'm sorry. I know it's around here somewhere. I'll bring it by your office when I find it."

He looks at me funny, but appreciates me going to him so he's not wasting his time. He leaves me thinking how close of a call that was. (I've had others before: boa feathers on my collared shirt; forgetting to silence inappropriate ringtones during client meetings; putting drawings my boss just gave me in a trunk full of empty beer cans.) Not sure what I would have said, but if we hadn't been so busy, the interaction would have ended either in a mountain of awkwardness or one hell of an excuse on the spot.

It's 1:13 a.m. Bottle swigs help but I'm still far from comfort, trying to relax and act like I belong in the middle of this dried-up creek bed. I've just met Antonio, and even though he's been nothing but welcoming, I'm still timid with him.

Tonight, we watch as the dancers go through their routines, sweating in rustic costumes under the June moonlight.

From humble speakers, the hot and brassy guitar buzz for the music video we'll film tomorrow echoes through this enchanting, central Texas ranch. And combat boots and bare feet slam on the sand again and again in rhythmic, crunching thuds while fingers appear and disappear from glistening, outstretched palms. Once they've implanted the sequences in their muscle memory, the dancers go to their tents to change and sleep for fewer hours than they need, while some of the crew and extras lie on the cooling sand that hugs them in soft and unique indentations. I can't exactly place it, but using rocks, sticks, hands, and voices as impromptu instruments to orchestrate unplugged versions of some of our favorite songs produces an experience somewhere between ecstasy and pure bliss. Sitting in this creek, I'm halfway through the change now. I don't know it yet, but the decision has been made at the fork. I've turned my back on security and money, and I'm moments away from sprinting down the path toward spontaneity and wonder.

It's 10:15 a.m. Room after room is empty. The equipment spaces and systems my firm helped design and implement in this facility are gone. The only remnants of our work are engineering drawings back home in our office's basement and buttprints from laid-off employees on the seats my boss and I pass by; people whose company, decades ago, put too many eggs in one basket. On the march through the main corridor, we shake our heads at process area after process area, each one more desolate than the last. Of the rooms that do have activity, half do so only because of demolition teams or groups of engineers and supervisors standing unfortunately close to tired operators and machines, talking relocation or how to scale down.

The last wisps of these broken dreams linger through the empty halls as water droplets fall from soaked hardhat sweatbands, wet with the toil of overworked, lifeless men. I cringe at the burden of the workers providing for their families and see them trudging around year after year in these once-illustrious rooms, only to fade and disappear into the white, sanitized walls. These men and women who gave their lives to the corporate world have now become somber and silent; yet the lights still flicker and the air-conditioning rumbles on, supporting ghosts of the past and a last ditch effort to save it all. If you take a big whiff in these buildings, you can almost smell the 1980s, while CEOs and CFOs across the nation cling to their glory days with as much vigor as they do their cigars, shoe shines, and limousine expediencies.

The state of these halls has become the norm. All over the world are these massive buildings filled with hundreds or thousands of people—half what there used to be—who sit in their cubes day after day, uninspired, doing nothing except checking fantasy teams. The only hope of salvation is punching the clock on Friday afternoon, on our way to suckle on Bud Light's aluminum teat, ranting about our bosses or how work could be better if only we were in charge. Fast-forward to Sunday and we've drank our weekend away, but there's still beer in the fridge and no sense in watching the game sober. So let's keep the coals burning through the binge.

But the reality that it's all born from the trickle-down is what truly makes me depressed.

It's 5:06 a.m. Yogis, artists, dancers, filmmakers, students, musicians, an administrative assistant, massage therapists, and a mechanical engineer are running around frantically, making sure they have their costumes and faces on, ready to go. The lead artist paints me with precise strokes, but thanks to a body that usually runs hot, I know it'll be smeared all over my forehead in an hour. The artist moves on to his next subject, and the production team reminds us that we need to be on the Rock by 5:45 a.m. to get ready for the first shots at the golden hour. This is crucial, they say, so we all help each other out with paint, wardrobe, Rock coordination, props, instruments, and bringing as much bottled water as we can. Dancers are going through intricate steps at the last minute, and I bask in the addictive chaos.

Running late, the director yells "grab everything you can and hike," and everyone starts the dawn trek. Along the way, the weathered and knife-edged scallops of the thrift store combat boots pierce into the tops of my ankles. Our trail goes through a second dried-up creek, over fallen trees, and up the final slants to the Rock, but there's no pain or anything left now that will stop me from seeing this break all the way through. I've come to terms with needing this in my life. I feel so ready, so willing. I feel like this is progress somehow.

By the time we get to the Rock, I'm in a full sweat and there's no doubt that blood is smudged on the boot shafts and running down my ankles, but all that fades away when we reach the flat top and I look over the reddish brown and green terrain touched with withering shadows and budding, morning rays. I'm imbued with pristine energy while a friend turns to me and smiles. "You have paint all up and down your face. Let me help you."

I do have paint all over my face. And it feels wonderful. Because on this Rock I'm free. In frayed but flowing garb, tattered sashes, even the combat boots, for some reason I feel like this is right. I feel lighter, more like myself. It's still a uniform, but it's much closer to my true identity (whatever that is) than button-downs and slacks.

For so long, I've put on a mask for client interaction, and I have to admit that it's begun to eat at me. There's great admiration for a few clients here and there, but for the most part I've become this Dillard's robot for people who care about me far, far less than they care about their bottom line. And after all of it, there's no appreciation, only cordiality when projects do go well.

Here on this Rock there are no hidden agendas. No fake interest in order to climb the ladder. No meaningless *how's the weather down there* dialogue. We're all here because the music speaks to us, and we share the common goal of helping to create superb art. The euphoric feeling I get on this Rock, seeing people from all walks of life, working, sweating, bleeding together, just to capture this moment of sunshine, dancing, music, and new friendships, is all I need. Throughout the filming, dancers' feet are aching, my friends' knees are getting bruised, and I'm pretty sure there's a few ounces of my life force pooling in my left boot, but we would all do this again, any day of the week, for free. This opportunity feels like the release I've been waiting for.

It's 2:00 p.m. I'm just finishing a fourth redo on a spreadsheet of project man-hours when an e-mail chimes from a client telling me to figure out a way to lower the construction cost again, even if that could mean making the manufacturing space for their sterile product less clean. Just another money-driven decision that handcuffs talent and quality to go on top of all the others I've seen since my days as a green-hat engineering intern.

Before this cube I worked at a chemical plant in southern Louisiana, helping with heat transfer equations and capstone projects in collaboration with a local college and the higher-ups in the buildings across the lake. My second week in, I opened my eyes midway through fighting off a lunch coma to catch my boss standing just inside the doorway. For several seconds, he only looked at me in harsh silence. "Welp, the union's done. Tomorrow the picket goes up, and the plant manager will organize us in shifts." I could tell he was slightly relieved, because he now had an out on the projects he was behind on. But I had to choose: part ways and end my internship with no hard feelings, or stay the course, attend the prep meeting tomorrow for the salaried (interns were regarded as such) and ride out the strike. I chose the latter and wouldn't second guess myself until the seventh straight night of sleeping in my office on a noisy, second-hand, polyester cot that from head to toe sagged half a foot in the middle. I was young and in my best physical health, but a summer spent with my body in a U shape made my neck and shoulders consistently ache, and that wouldn't even scratch the surface of what I would end up going through.

Two-thirds chose the other side of the fence, so the white collars and scabs were split into three shifts of eight days each. Before the sun rose on the last day of each shift, the salaried parking lot would uncoil like a fat, groggy snake into a fifteen-minute long convoy of metal that was yelled and spat at by the blue collars on COBRA as our cars crawled across the picket line one by one.

The four days off were just enough to balance out the eight straight of turning wrenches on Kynar pipes filled with acid while wearing clunky brain buckets, grime-coated gloves with even worse insides, coveralls of FRP, and another layer of clothes stained with salt underneath. The summer was brutal, but the heat we really felt came off the flame arrestors and bus-sized boilers we had to cuddle up against while prying off lug nuts with tools as long as our legs. I was only twenty-two, but many of the remaining employees doing this were over sixty.

As we rotated valves, we rotated responsibilities within our team's designated area of the plant. The short straw of the lot was the "bottoms" plant where the sewage from the rest of the facility would go. It was a terrible, terrible place that processed the sludgiest, filthiest, thickest paste of caustic soda, vinyl chloride, and a plethora of other aggressive mixes, the smell of which has remained with me all these years later. I would imagine it's similar to putting your face inside a bag of a dog's hot excrement and taking a deep, lengthy sniff. But afterwards, you're not done. You can't take it away from your face to give yourself a breather. You keep your nose in that bag. You keep it in there and you keep it deep. You keep it way down in there, and you breathe again, because there's no escaping. You breathe and breathe and you breathe, steaming poop an inch or two from your nostrils, and in doing that for an hour or two, you'll start to understand the everyday knee-deep of that job. It was one of the few places I've been where I felt sick just from standing in the vicinity.

And I've never been paid more.

I thought it would get better after college graduation and an industry switch, but I now attend meetings where egos butt heads so much that the only decisions they can make are placing blame on someone or something else or the scheduling of the next meeting. And I regularly watch my projects hit standstills while my $120-an-hour billing rate keeps eating away budgets every second.

Back in the chains at my desk, my disposition turns stormy and impulsive.

Another e-mail comes in. Bad news again. My back hurts. Not sure when that started. It's worse than the testicle pain—which ended up a benign fluke—so I can't push this one into the background.

Don't get me wrong, I like my company. Some parts aren't as good as others, but it's one of the most laid-back engineering firms one could hope for. I consider myself lucky to have contributed to a few pacesetting projects, putting something good into the world, and to have learned under some brilliant people. Still, I have visions of clients from across the U.S. yanking on a giant chain leash, wrenching my neck until the popping and crunching of bone can be heard. *We need it tomorrow, even though we won't do anything with it for weeks.* Two of my coworkers have quit because they had chest pains from the stress. At the chemical plant, another older coworker had his face sprayed with chlorine gas (a work-related safety incident) because, in his twelfth hour of working in the oppressive humidity, he just wanted to finish the maintenance job so he could go back to his office to eat and relax. My last boss was hospitalized twice, and after getting back to health, still overworks himself like nothing happened. Any given day, I'll knock on his door to ask how it's going, and a part of me dies inside when not ever taking his eyes off his screen he says, "Oh, I'm just workin' for a living." And I've had a nagging knot of stress between my shoulder blades that's been getting worse by the day for I don't know how long. I've seen hundreds, thousands of people that are completely beat down by their jobs. Some of them don't even drink or smoke and they still have hangovers, solely from the best days at work. And in any given facility, nametag protocol is to reuse pictures taken upon hiring, keeping haggard, potbellied people wearing laminated versions of themselves twenty years younger. *This is just the way the system works; these are necessary, soul-sucking jobs that people just have to fill.*

Is there really not a better way? Does the satisfaction of a paycheck trump our ability and responsibility? Trying and challenging workdays that make it tough to get out of bed are inevitable, but they don't have to be continuous. Every day doesn't have to be a cesspool of agony into which we pour alcohol, cocaine, and pain pills. There's much better work to be done. We should all just have a giant meeting one day to figure out how we can change the way our jobs are run and raise the happiness bar. Wouldn't that be something.

It's 3:00 p.m. I sneak out of work to prevent a panic attack, and go to a park near my place—one of my sacred spaces. The openness and peacefulness always calm me down. I run and run across the park like a gazelle in the Serengeti, watching people fly kites, play with their children, hug each other. All of these people beam, practice, enjoy life, and I used to look at them and think they were wastes of space. *You're only happy because you aren't a productive member of society. You don't have*

to shoulder the burden. I used to think they were going nowhere in life, but right now I can't help but think maybe that's me. Maybe all of this slaving away, seldom seeing the light of day, just so the numbers in my bank account and 401(k) get higher is not being productive. Am I just fast-forwarding through most of my life? I'll hit stop when I'm sixty-five or older, my body broken, my mind fatigued, and then that's when I can enjoy life. That's when I can travel. Right. I'd much rather travel the world and climb mountains when I'm sixty-eight, not twenty-eight. That makes sense.

My chest is hurting again and my back is right there with it. Am I actually having a panic attack? In a park? I can't believe it's come to this. Is it because my projects have gotten that much worse or is it because of the glimpses of humanity's freedom around me? Whichever it is, I can't keep this up. It's making me crazy. I don't have enough energy for both. One must be let go. *Wait, this is crazy. Don't be hasty. This is just a bad day. Tomorrow will be better.*

It's 8:06 p.m. "Fi-re whip! Fi-re whip! Fi-re whip!" The barbarous men and skimpy women that have stumbled over to drape themselves along the fences yell their simple drunken demand, but Ava's shouts with hints of childhood rise above it all. Before the high swoon of the bagpipes and marching drums, before the ground is lit alive, before the launching sticks glimmer with fountains of blue and green sparks, the chanting of the crowd echoes almost demonically through the shadows at a silent man waiting in the middle of the field. The flick from a lighter shoots down in a line and curls around at the bottom before fully illuminating the man who now swings his snake of fire. Great sweeping circles of blue, magenta, and white speed up and up, and the racing curlicue shoots the fuel down the fall, hits the cracker, and is flung out, whacking the air in front of the crowd with an elephant-sized fireball. The man continues to lash the air with Z's and S's and manages to keep his clothing from catching as he intertwines his entire body with the blazing whip. Ava gives an approving yelp and whistle, and her fingers slide between mine, sending a meteorotic and lustful charge up my spine. After the whipping is finished, the crowd is rambunctious and applause takes over the scene. It all dies down again for a few minutes until we see two more flickers and then two flaming snakes in the middle of the field.

By the end of the night, we gather the rest of our friends to head back through the camps and sprawled-out parties to our cars. A hunchback drags a bucket past us through the mud. He shifts his body at an angle to look up to us and repeatedly says, "May you reproduce multiple times to beautiful music." As we leave the festival grounds, my phone vibrates with a calendar invite from my boss for a 9:00 a.m. meeting tomorrow morning.

It's 4:00 p.m. The sound of blades pulverizing coffee beans in my hands hypnotizes me. The smell spurs me. I can already taste the coffee. I'll be sure to have two more cups before the end of the night because I have to make up the two hours I spent reflecting in the park, and I can't work late tomorrow because of three o'clock happy hour. God, I can't wait to be so drunk and out of this place—this eight- by eight-foot cell where I've suddenly become five years older. It's all I can focus on.

I take the black bean juices of vengeance and walk down Misery Lane, trying to avoid eye contact from coworkers on my way back to my cube. I flick my mouse, brace myself, and look at Outlook from the corner of squinting eyes, waiting for a rhythmic repetition of punches to the face.

Sixteen e-mails. Son of a bitch. . . . Most of them aren't too bad, but then—

Then, the atom bomb.

A client is blaming me for a miscalculation on a project I submitted drawings (stamped and signed) for two years ago. I spend the next hour looking at archived e-mails, but all I can think about is that I should be doing something else. I have so many other deadlines this week, but "this is a crucial client," my boss always says, so I know I'll have to stay another hour later tonight.

Finally, I find the e-mail. The client told me to use the numbers I used. Awesome . . . awesome, awesome, awesome.

I craft a short but polite response, and by the end, it adds up to $100 worth of time (legacy discount) that I can't charge because the project was closed over two years ago. Because of helping someone who accused me of screwing them, my total billable percentage is gonna go down. I keep fixating on the client's original, crass e-mail and come to the scary realization that this will never stop. It won't be better next year. It won't be better ten years from now. I'll be doing the same thing, just with bigger problems and more bouts with stress-induced pain. With better technology, clients will just want drawings and reports even faster, with more demands and less politeness. They'll never back down.

And here my hand is forced. I make my decision—a decision that I've been on the path to for years but is completely shocking to me.

I fucking quit.

A fierce flood rushes through my brain, but I don't know what other end to meet. My dad will be devastated, having spent so much money on my education. What will my boss think, having spent so much time mentoring me? Just knowing how disappointed he'll be . . . I don't want to see his eyes when I tell him. I close mine and lay my head on my desk. After several minutes, I stand up to look over the farm at my coworkers crunching numbers in between glances at the time in the bottom-right corner of their screens. My good friend Magnus is drawing at a frantic pace in his cube, having no clue what just happened fifteen feet to his right. *Man. Give me strength for that conversation.*

There's no way I'm staying late now. I leave work still heavily surprised, but lighter than I've felt in years. I drive home underneath a freedom sky, and not even rush hour can phase me. I spend a day getting used to this choice, making sure: this is what I want, right?

The next day, I call my mom and dad; they're naturally shocked and silently confused, respectively. *Has our boy gone crazy?* I explain my feelings and considerations—everything—until I break down. I tell them about the near panic attack, the ball of stress. I tell them I'm not happy, but I can infer from their responses that money is their top concern. I make sure they know this won't affect their pockets because of the backup plan I've been brewing for a long time now but never thought would need to happen this soon. But sometimes, you gotta take your blind leap. Sometimes the unknown can be comforting because it can only be better than where you've come from. There's no room to go back this time.

Yes. I want this.

ALL THE BUTTERFLIES

On our late afternoon descent, a phalanx of purples, dreams triangles, oranges, and jellyfish races above us, fanning out from one horizon to another, never to be seen again. But riding in on the coattails to begin the opus of daylight is a new angelic horde of labyrinthine patterns and entangled rapture that's destined to give the wolves yet another rich, chromatic performance. And soon after, the ever-succulent climax will be brought on by the halved sun in a fast shrink, wishing us good luck and good evening along the way.

As we make it back to camp, Diego looks to have one foot in the animal realm with the other about to join. He and Cyrus sprawl out in lawn chairs over cracked and burdened dirt while Antonio and I plop down on a blanket freshly rolled out yet already littered with handfuls of spiny burr. Antonio says it's a good time to be acquainted with our guide for the evening, so he asks Cyrus to read the medicine card. I'm not sure why they picked Armadillo earlier, but it will certainly pave the way for what comes for me tonight. I wonder what I would be engrossed in right now had that card not been read, or if I had missed this trip. Would the same experience be waiting for me, just a little further down the road, or was this instance, this combination of elements just right that it could only happen this way?

The finer details have been coming up more and more. Maybe subtlety is an acquired taste with older age, or maybe I had been so wrapped up in my cubicle and timesheets filled to the brim with Post-it notes and coffee grounds that I couldn't see beyond the daily tasks and liquid motivation. Ever since I quit, all these little nuances now have the ability to set the tone for the rest of the day. It was hard to shift my focus during the Big Rush, but now when I sit back and just be for five minutes, the subliminal flow never ceases to surprise. If I pay attention, if I really concentrate on living and the incredible amount of events it's taken to get to any given situation, every moment can harbor childbirth, a Las Vegas win streak, the crunching of a bull rider's spine, a disastrous breakup, your mother and father fighting, fire crackling, a deaf girl hearing her voice for the first time through technological means, golden love. It's somewhere down in there, you just gotta sift through all the layers.

There's a girl I know who makes her scratch from painting murals for local businesses and spaces for children. Though it's in her personal collection that you'll find the real gems: old couches busting with white stuffing that are stacked and strewn about the yard, the smudged piano with angled sharps and flats left out in the rain, and the splattered and dripping wedding dress and tuxedo in filled-out frontals with no man or woman underneath. There's a bed, a dog, the everyday, the unsung constants of our lives. There's a beauty she brings out in the mundane, and she's one of the happiest people I know.

Having found the Armadillo medicine card, Cyrus apologizes beforehand if his mouth becomes a bowl of gravy and mashed potatoes. As he stares at the card, Antonio looks up at the sunset clouds whipping into each other like white and yolk, while I gaze entranced at the plaid blanket beneath me—reds and greens ebbing and flowing into and out of each other. Cyrus maintains his silence, piquing our interest. He rubs his stomach and fingers the bottom button of his shirt, working to conjure energy. He tries to breathe out gently, building up his strength. He's still just sitting there in preparation while butterflies dance inside me, their wings gliding across my midsection in a frenzy of Rorschachs in flight.

Finally, he lets out a long sigh and begins: *"Armadillo wears its armor on its back, its medicine a part of its body. Its boundaries of safety are a part of its total being. Armadillo can roll into a ball and never be penetrated by enemies.*

"What a gift it is to set your boundaries so that harmful words or intentions just roll off. Your lesson is in setting up what you are willing to experience. If you do not wish to experience feeling invaded, just call on Armadillo medicine.

"A clue to how to proceed is to make a circle on a piece of paper and see it as a medicine shield. In the body of the shield, write all that you are desiring to have, do, or experience. Include all things that give you joy. This sets up boundaries that allow only these chosen expediencies to be a part of your life. These boundaries become a shield that wards off the things which are undesirable to you. The shield reflects what you are and what your will is to others on an unconscious level. Outside of the shield you may put what you are willing to experience by invitation only, for

example a visit from a long lost relative, or criticism from friends, or people needing handouts. . . .

"How you react in any circumstance has to do with your ability to be objective. You cannot be objective if you cannot tell where the other person's personality stops and where yours begins. If you have no boundaries, you are like a sponge. It will seem as if all the feelings in a room full of people must be yours. Ask yourself if you are really feeling depressed, or if this feeling actually belongs to the person you are talking to. Then allow Armadillo's armor to slide in between, giving you back your sense of self."

Cyrus pauses and cracks his back and neck a few times.

"Man," Antonio says. "And that's just regular Armadillo, right?"

"Yes, sir. Now here's Contrary Armadillo. *"Go ahead, roll up and hide. This, sarcastically, is the message of reversed Armadillo. You may think the only way to win in your present situation is to hide or to pretend that you are armor-coated and invincible, but this is not the way to grow. It is better to open up and find the value and strength of your vulnerability. You will experience something wonderful if you do.*

"Vulnerability is the key to enjoying the gifts of physical life. In allowing yourself to feel, a myriad of expressions are made available. For instance, a true compliment is an admiration flow of energy. If you are afraid of being hurt and are hiding from feeling anything, you will never feel the joy of admiration from others.

"The key is in allowing Armadillo to help you to stop hiding and to use Armadillo's armor to deflect negative energies. In this way, you are able to accept or reject any feeling, action, or energy flow without having to hide from it.

"The underside of Armadillo is soft, but its armor will protect this softness if the boundaries are in place. Hiding from your true feelings and fearing failure or rejection will amplify your need for cast-iron protection.

You have the power to rid yourself of these doubts and to touch the deepest part of beingness. You will know you are doing the right thing. Whether it is communicating, or painting, or surfing—the creation belongs to you. The only real rejection is in not trying break out of the armor you have used to protect yourself. Is the armor now becoming a jail, and your fears the jailer?"

Cyrus tries that last paragraph again, slow and peculiar—"The underside of Armadillo is soft . . ."—but he never finishes. I can only assume that, like my mad-dancer butterflies, the words are beginning to flutter on the page. Cyrus closes the book, runs his fingers over the cover, and looks at each of us, his face contorting. His lips swim across each other, somehow managing to resemble a trembling but happy grin. "I just . . . I just need to stop."

"It's cool, man," Antonio laughs. "We got you. We all doin' the damn thing together."

"Yeah, I just want to enjoy this with you guys and relax," Cyrus says. "I just want to live." And with that, the wild man turns simple. Five words of no more than four letters each pierce through me like slender, agile wings knifing through the sky. After his words soak into the camp, Cyrus puts the medicine book away with the sun, making way for night to be born all around us.

It couldn't have come at a better time because under most circumstances I never want to vomit in the eyesight of my friends. I've already warned the guys, "I'm a puker, so don't worry if I sneak off somewhere in a hurry." I also like to retch in exotic or intricate locations. I figure, if I'm going to do such a foul, violent act, I might as well do it in a provocative setting that has some sort of visual pleasure. So with the butterflies whispering of evils in my stomach, and knowing the food exodus will be freak-out-free, I begin to survey the surroundings.

Night has taken a fast, firm hold over this anxious camp. We're nestled up against a shaggy, meager cliff, lined with saplings, bleak briar, and the dead foliage that will soon become the sacrificial kindling. A low, hissing waterfall in the distance, chilling water slipping through rocks in the rills, a convoluted root system all around us, and a clean, flat floor for the future flames—this is the setting for what will wind up as the most important campfire in my twenty-eight years of existence.

The creek bank? No.

Behind the cave? Too far.

Up near the bluff? We're all downstream

A group of three tree trunks seemingly growing out of the same hole in the ground? That'll work.

I'm all systems go as Diego starts to talk about girls and living vicariously. I excuse myself and bound up the hill, through thorn and root, agitating the evil inside me, excited for the relief I know I'll feel when I deliver my brooding darkness unto the mouth of life. I make it to the throng of trunks, brace my increasingly rotund body with the two close ones, and look down upon nature's nexus to find a receptacle of dirt and grub.

After a few vicious convulsions, the murk and poison wells up from my stomach and froths out of my throat into nightfall, tasting like the whites of orange peels on my lips, both surprising me and not. Another rush shoots up inside of me and comes forth with a hint of bubble-purple that slides down the bark. I wonder if these trees have ever felt this experience before.

I empty myself a few more times, each heave waking me up more and more, bringing my senses to novel levels of acuteness. But then I look down to see only a small puddle of semi-digested matter in the gorge—mostly orange, mostly disappointing.

"That's it?" I feel cheated, like I had so much more to offer, but I'm thankful for what did come out. I'll leave the rest for later.

My shoulder drops onto the left trunk, and I wearily look up at the soft colors of dusk, trying to bring back calmness, peace. My nose whistles while I breath in, and the surface of my skin interlaces with that of the cypress next to me—the blanket of bark that enables my fractal shade ladies to withstand hundreds, even thousands of years to be our epic and stoic protectors, the janitors of the air.

My friends' voices break up my conversation with the three trees and the pit they make. I wish I could cuddle up in this bosom for longer, but the butterflies have taken a nap, and it's time to return to my fellow wolves.

I rejoin the animal to find heavy smoke floating in front of Diego's face, his cigarette puffs carrying lessons with them, each smoke cloud a piece of advice. He offers me one but I decline even though it smells so damn good. Instead, I grab a water bottle, and because dried puke is the worst, empty it all over my face while Diego talks of his life experiences with humans that are penis-free. The oldest of the group, and the most grounded, he speaks in a stream of anecdotes and on-the-mark banter after every pull of his magic stick.

"Because you don't want to have sex with her, you will have sex with her. And I shall watch you. I shall watch you free your penis inside of her."

As he puffs wisdom all over our faces, I weigh the idea of him being one of the main characters in our next project. With his shaved head, brown skin, small eyes, and almost elegant demeanor, he looks right at home in this forest, offering mini-enlightenments like a giant turtle in meditation, sucking on a pipe with eyes semi-sedated.

"You know, back in the cave, no one really painted females. That's a damn shame. Us males hogging all the history. Even now, you see it with the Bechdel test."

"Ah . . . wait. What's it again?" Cyrus asks.

"A work of fiction's gotta have a Sabrina and a Jenny. To pass the test they gotta talk to each other. And it has to be about something besides a man and his honey buns."

"That's right," Cyrus says. "And how many pass?"

"Maybe half. Man. I'm so tired of Hollywood being such a gigantic sausage fest. I mean, we know everyone's degree of separation from Kevin Bacon but—"

"Hey! Watch yourself!" I say. "I love you man, but Kevin Bacon's performance in *Tremors* is absolute poetry."

"I know it is," Diego says. "You're right, you're right . . . But how many times have you heard a plot where three guys fight over an airhead? The men carry the story while the girl just sits there being all pretty. But she's more than that. She's passionate, smart, independent. She's a bearer of life!"

"Womens is such beautiful creatures," Antonio says.

"You're damn right," I say. "I think we'll see a powerful woman come to lead us. And soon too. I'm not Ray Kurzweil or Punxsutawney Phil, but 'dreams do not lack—'"

"Oh my God!"

We all swivel in unison toward Antonio, but he's already sprung up and jogging toward his girlfriend's car in a low and awkward bustle. Twenty or so yards away, he settles into his perch behind the vehicle: elbows on the hood, butt sticking way out, hands supporting his face—a weird position to see anyone assume. He sits there like a mischievous thespian, almost hiding behind the car but captivated by something in the distance.

"What's over there?" Cyrus shouts.

"The moon," he says. "It's so vivid. Look at it, playing with them clouds. Look-look-look-look-look." He giggles to himself, and then giggles harder. "Guys, guys, guys . . . giggling has four g's in it."

Antonio's giggling starts my own and soon my abs are tearing apart. On his left, Diego gazes at the moon, then looks back to Antonio, in playful, judging bewilderment.

"Why are you standing like this?" Diego asks.

"I . . . I don't fucking know, dude!" Antonio says. "Just look at the moon. Don't look at how I stand. It doesn't . . . These things don't matter now." Antonio buries his head in his hands as his giggling continues, and I pat him on the back in reassurance before I go on my hunt.

Up ahead before the main road, there's a clearing that I decide to make my way for because sometimes I can become a perfectionist and Antonio's view just isn't cutting it. A few of my friends say I'm hard to please, to which I reply, "only during times of absolute necessity," and while the subtle game between the moonlight and the tree branches is great, right now I need to get as much sun-moon juice as I can, to feel that full reflective power. *No offense, Antonio. A wolf has his needs.*

I awkwardly dash along the creek to get out from under the canopy, almost tripping on brighter and brighter objects because the moon is not empty; it's about to overflow and our modest creek-side plot is the only receptacle to dump into.

My goodness.

I make it to the clearing, and a commanding spotlight—complete with the dull gray parts inside—bathes me with unabated, long-distance connection, the power of which leads me to squint in the night. It's as if the moon has pushed its way to sit in front of the clouds, to shine only on this small stretch of land. And in my periphery, I notice everything around—the creek, the short precipice, the woodland in the distance—is lit up like a carnival; it might as well be day.

"Can you believe we landed on that thing?" Cyrus asks, scaring me into a full body flinch. His face a few inches away from my shoulder, even the lunar reflections in his eyes are intense. "Like, one night, a couple dudes were looking at the moon and the louder one asks his friend, 'Jes' how much you wan' bet we gon' walk on that moon up yonder? A hunderd? Two hunderd?'"

"Aw, hell, Skeeter," I say, playing along. "I reckon it's the moonshine talkin' 'gain. Nah how in the hayl you figgur we gon' do that?"

"Oh, that thar's easy. All we needa do is get that ole UFO over'n Roswull, load 'er up with some kerosene, whip us up some o' dem science fiction suits and helmets, and we'd be offta that ole rock up thar in no time."

"Yer crazier'n a shithouse fly, Skeeter. Even crazier'n a road-runnin' lizard. . . . Well, I needa go drain this here lizard, if'n ya catch ma drift."

"If'n you jes' peein' 'n' ain't pukin', then tha's all right I guess. Catch ya on down that trail, but I tell ya what boy . . .

we gon' walk on that moon. Yessir. You can bet your purdy white ass on that."

I'm not sure why we acted the first-moon-walking conversation out as hillbillies, but gosh darn it, that's how it came out. And when that happens, you run with it. You run with it until them cows come home.

Cyrus joins the others back at the campfire and I find a good spot to take a leak. Out over the edge of the flat, this weird appendage hangs off my body. There's nothing elegant about it, is there? More ridiculous and silly than necessary as an evolutionary device. And if I'm being honest, when you're way down in the rabbit hole, he's a bit hard to work with because you can't feel the difference between him and your hand. Instead, you struggle with this singular, shape-shifting mass in front of you, trying to get it to do the distinct movements you want. It makes it a problem keeping your hands and pants dry, so I go hands-free; accuracy just isn't worth it out here. But after getting all this out of the way, the hardest part is that I can't tell when I'm finished. With the developing minutiae going on around me, it's tough to concentrate on what should be automatic bodily functions. So much so that a full bladder and the closing off of my urethra aren't isolated feelings. But what is a man to do besides sucking it up and winging it?

I'm about to commit when the bogs and loblollies start whispering of the catastrophe that once happened along the length of this brook. Back before humans were humans, but not before Tommy the Amoeba, every tree was trampled and uprooted around this old quagmire by something big that came through the basin.

Whuup.

I start peeing, but as I feel the rush and release of urine, a wave sneaks up on me and kicks in hard, spurring me to blow the more stubborn bulk of my last meal out into a semi-circle beside my feet. *Ah . . . there's the rest of it.* Standing up straight again, my eyes roll and slide around my head and my body becomes loose, galvanizing my senses again and lubricating my cells. I'm not proud of it, but I've been a habitual back, neck, and knuckle cracker since I was twelve or thirteen years old—something I'm sure will catch up to me in the future. For me, this gives my joints a rest, as if not just the mind but the body, too, expands and makes room for all of those muscles inflamed with stress. With the extra space, I arch my back and my neck so that my hair falls on my trapezius. My neck curves forward and my shoelaces catch my eye, reflecting electric in the beam of the moon. But no . . .

I look up and I'm not here anymore. Here on earth, I mean.

The contrast and sharpness of my surroundings have been scrolled up to the maximum end of the bar, and like the hue of dusk in a video game, there's a few wonky qualities, but the shade lines travel crisp across the sky, marking the supernova highways and shortcuts for the interstellar ships to cruise on. An overwhelming feeling of superstrings and superclusters hits me, and I ride the dark waves of the cosmos to find myself regenerated as a starchild on a planet far from here. I pick my feet up, put them down a few times to get my bearings, scrape the dirt around with my shoes, and realize maybe I'm not as far from home as first perceived. There's no way to know for sure, but a biting gale comes forth and the way the brook, soil, and atmosphere surge over each other like rings of opposing storms reminds me of Jupiter. The dead swamp-like roots and brush near me are alien, but as on earth, life here likes to play with itself, chase itself around, like the wee fur ball scurrying after obscured rodents along the dark side of the creek bank I've been dumping urine into.

Jeffrey—the spry fur ball—isn't used to the warmth and scampers past the car into the leaves at the base of the cliff face, trying to find a cold patch. *My apologies, little guy. We'll try to find you a cold swell here, soon.*

The Jupiter sky becomes electric and amplified, meaning the wolves are in for a long, graphic evening. Cutting midnight blue and sharp across the terrain, the hue from earlier isn't strange anymore. And the stars shine arc flash white, especially after all the Jupiter aircrafts have gone home, running hot from their daily commute. Palpable is a weak word for the intensity level so far. Already, I realize things aren't gonna be normal the rest of the night. This trip won't be either.

My stream turns to droplets—my cue to do the ritualistic shake dance.

Wait, am I done? I can't tell. My hands are wet. *Wait . . . are they?*

I just have to trust my muscle memory and tell myself that I don't really care. This is how it's supposed to go. I tuck in and try to zip up, but my jean zipper laughs at me with infinite teeth. I pull up and up, but there's no satisfying stopping feeling. I struggle for a bit longer and manage to zip the loose flap of my boxers halfway into the teeth.

I walk back giggling, not totally sure why, but back at the campfire, the guys are waiting for me with the craziest grins. Cyrus is as far back in his chair as he can be, running his hands through his hair and licking his lips. I'm so glad he came. A group of four is always a good number to have when you're out here in the singular mass; it really balances everything out.

Diego and Antonio lounge, too, as if they've just punched the clock after a long life's work, making the prospect of resting my legs seem so enticing that I give it a try.

Damn. It's beyond my wildest dreams. It'll take a miracle or all the energy of the universe to get me up again.

We all feel the first draft swirl in. Antonio says it's time, but to Cyrus, our Eagle Scout, it's not the time at all. He's as present as can be, just not capable of the task we need to have happen. Antonio looks him over and gets it—telepathy levels and the hive mind now approach measurability. He nods, gets up, and starts without Cyrus. Log, kindling, stick teepee, more kindling, matches, smoke, magic breath, first few sparks, more magic.

Fire. Sweet, miraculous, enchanting, recapturing, holy dip-my-body-in-eternity fire. El Fuego. What would life be without it? It wouldn't. Not in this universe. Everything revolves around it. It's the Prime Mover, the Destructor. For the next five hours, it'll have me fully invested. It'll wrap me up and care for me—like a mother.

It will also be my end.

Cyrus reflects on the moon. "It's like a bounce board for the earth," he says.

With beads of sweat on his forehead from his great deeds, Antonio is sitting back down when I notice that my jeans—preferring a more fluid appearance—are rippling under my hands. I'm not sure where the holes begin or end. My skin feels jean-y. My jeans feel skin-y. I know Antonio and Cyrus are saying something about the moon, but I'm captivated by the activity on Jupiter. I hope Jeffrey's all right. Poor little guy. He must be burning up. I look over my shoulder, back to the moon.

The surface filters are gone, but I try to remain plugged in.

"Man, the moon is like . . . what are those fabric discs you use to reflect sunlight off of?" I ask. "Like in a photo shoot?"

Antonio squints at me. "You mean a . . . bounce board?"

"Yeah, it's like the moon is one huge bounce board aiming at earth."

Cyrus and Antonio look at me, trying to cover up their confusion. My mind catches up and I finally realize why.

"Oh, that's what you just said, huh?" Cyrus and Antonio stop holding in their laughter. "Damn, I'm sorry, dude! I'm sorry, guys. I'm a little uh . . . well, you know."

We sit in a rare stretch of silence as the rest of the kindling burns through, but the main log is playing hard to get and left mostly unscathed. Somehow, Diego can still move, and does something about it, disappearing into the forest to search for more wonderful tree fingers. *Bless you, kind sir.* I've been focusing on the fireplace for only a few minutes, but it plays out like forever in my mind, until a want for heat is all I know now because I've forgotten all about the moon.

I swear I hear beating drums from somewhere beyond the streamlets when I see light from the jungle as Diego emerges fast from the woods with clumps of fuel in his hands. In front of him, a loud spectrum of times to come illuminates his amble. His headlamp shapes him into a space-age, apocalyptic survivor, returning from the long journey of foraging for leaves, twigs, and time to rekindle my now cold heart.

He feeds the smoldering log, leading jagged light to burst from the sanctum, and in this time of renewed warmth, I reach my ultimate being.

61

DRENCHED IN ELECTRICITY

The wax and wane of the fire embers hold me to a trance, and with their hypnotic surging comes ineffability:

A ∞ Ꮐ ⁞⁞ Ӂ ◯ Å ‡ ▦

ᚻ Δ Σ Ω π Ⴘ ❁ ⛫

† ₪ ♀ ♂ ☼ Z

A shock wave of vitality hurtles through me, forever altering my concept of the oranges and yellows, the campsite and beyond. I'm exposed to an underlying loop of creation that possesses all points. In this singularity of that which is dark, everything is continuously born and destroyed in perfect balance, leaving time as nothing more than a discarded veil.

The field of view and its cyclical process form a pixelated ocean of design, with disturbances not of time and space but of invention, meaning, and oneness. Each pixel, good or evil, rides the ripple of existence—the repeating tango of consciousness and unconsciousness.

It's as if I've pressed down hard on my eyelids and then opened my eyes. Those tracers, the little zigzag dots of light with angel hair tails, are all I see. And like tiny, intermittent black holes, they funnel into and out of themselves, like burning flowers blooming out of their points of origin, only to be sucked back in again.

Clarity and simplicity are the cornerstones of this reality. There is a universal power at work here all around us. It's right here for us, right now, and we all have access to it. We can catch and rein in this creativity and use it—like a pencil paintbrush, wakeboard, calculator, baseball, or handshake—to bring meaning to our life and others', to be beautiful, to love, to be loved, to be love. Whatever each of our imaginations can dream of or conjure up is here.

And we're all soaking in this malleable, ever-present pool. We're drenched in it. Drenched in this electricity of creativity.

The cognitive circuit couples me to each molecule. There's a sense that even the most insignificant or unfavorable point is necessary for all the others. My physical body feels like it's flickering, like a dinoflagellate, with the sheer gratitude of existence. And for the first time, I can see a glimpse of the real universe, in all its creativity. For the first time, I can see that the universe is creativity.

I am alive.

I completely surrender to the moment, but then again, maybe surrender is what brought this rapture to begin with. And then friendships, jobs, ideas, states of mind swoop in to appear in front of me, and my hands run over them like links on a chain, feeling every moment play out again. I've left them, but they're all still here and now, because I wouldn't be without them.

Individual breaths of information, the being and history behind each campsite component all dance in the smoke in front of me, then they shoot into me, because I'm a part of the network. The knowledge spreads like wild lightning inside my form, and I've never been more aware of being plugged in. The makeup on Lady Life's face disappears, and she is more beautiful and intricate than I've ever thought before— the incarnation of intertwingling order and chaos, the celestial blueprint.

How does this keep at the forefront? How do I make this apparent in every moment? *Stop.* I can't get ahead of myself. I have to just let this be. I can't be too superlative or whimsical. I need to be cognizant of the ground and the wolves around me. We're all different and observe accordingly.

And then . . . something. Something I've never felt—a whisper in the back of my head.

"Guys, I need light," I shout, interrupting Diego. "Does someone have a flashlight?"

"What?" Diego says. "What for?"

"I just got an idea. I don't know. I have to write it down."

"Seriously?" Cyrus asks. "Like, right now while we're—"

"Right now, fast." I get out of my chair. Cyrus leaps to his feet, and reaches into his pocket.

"Here, man, use mine," he says.

Thank you, Cyrus. Thank you more than you'll ever know. I rush to find my notepad in my tent and try to look for my pen. I kneel down and turn the flashlight on.

"Oh . . . my . . . God. . . . Are you guys seeing this?"

The flashlight looks like a submarine traversing the depths of our minds. Future beacons strobe past us as we're going through this tunnel. Bill Murray is driving. He's driving this submarine—probably using his witty humor for fuel.

"What are you doing? You're not writing!" Cyrus yells.

"Shit. Sorry!"

"No time for being sorry. Write!"

I find the pen, and I start throwing handwriting diarrhea all over the tent and notepad. I can't work the flashlight properly, I can't work my pen properly. *Shit!* I need to get this down while it's still in me. *Remember the thoughts. Remember the thoughts. What? No. I mean, just let it flow. Just let it flow. Calm down and steady your hand. Dammit! Just write. What the hell does any of this mean? I don't know. It doesn't matter if you can't read it right now. Just write. Can you feel these words? Can you feel these words?*

Can you feel these words?

"I feel like I'm watching like . . . I don't know . . . something being born right now," Cyrus says.

I can't think about that. Just get it out. Faster! This stupid flashlight, write it down now, writeitdownwriteitdown nownownownownow, thisdoesn'tevenmakesense, don't worry, just step aside for the message, let it flow through, I'm just a piece. Let what flow? This is gibberish. I'm just a means to an end. Shit. This is exhausting. Where does this all begin? Where does it end? I don't know. No one knows.

Okay. I think I'm done. Wait. I don't—. I guess we'll see in the morning. Damn, it's cold. Gotta get back to the fire.

A plume of quivering breath escapes in front of me.

"What? How do you . . . ? How does this work? Someone turn this off for me," I say, my mind completely devoid of common sense. I give up trying to turn the flashlight off and give it to Cyrus. He helps.

"You okay, dude?" he asks.

"Phheww. I don't know, man. I mean, yeah. I just need to get warm."

Sweet, sweet warmth. My legs feel like clouds right now, like tiny seraphim are carrying them along, yet I still manage to climb into my chair—a final resting place for my body, old and shed. Breath escapes again. This time it transforms into eyes. Not smoke. Not mist. Just eyes. And a whole mess of them. I look at the dirt—eyes. I look at the flaming logs—eyes. I look at the enveloping trees—eyes. I look at Diego's eyes. Only, there aren't two of them. I can count at least forty on his chin, cheeks, and ears. They're all eyes—and they're all looking at me. Thousands of eyes around me. The pupils are all the same—some sort of pixilated rainbow-kaleidescopic-space colors. From space. I've heard people talk about their third eye, but this is just silly.

Then, on top of everything else, something more potent, more concentrated takes hold.

THE UNDERBELLY OF ARMADILLO

Sitting back in my lawn chair, the universe funnels into me. This is the most concentrated power I've experienced, but the warmth totters precariously on the peak. The embers become ash just as fast as they became flame. Then my spine feels the crispness first; my shoulders are right behind. I want to spring up, to help swell the fire, but there's no way I can move these chicken, frigid limbs of mine. The chair—where my psyche now lies—grounds me until I am a part of it and what grows underneath.

I'm now at the mercy of my friends, shackled down and helpless like a baby. Why can't these embers become flames? Why won't they? The edge of the firelight loosens its grip on us and retreats back to nothing, and bite and gloom grow dense over the flat and leech into the earth. All I want is to spend the rest of my life in the hearth, this sphere, this magical, orange warmth orb.

And then a miracle happens. Now, inch by mystical inch, the warmth orb inflates for reasons I can't see. The edge crosses over my feet, my little toesies, and ecstasy ripens inside of me. It quells my fear to manageable levels, and in a few more moments, the nurturing ring turns my disposition to brilliance and wealth. I could live in these flames, the pointed, torrid tails scorching and thundering through my skin to the third movement of Beethoven's Piano Sonata no. 17 in D Minor.

The only two concepts in this world I'm greedy for are love and warmth. As my three friends trade adventures back and forth, I lust deeper for the latter, ruminating on the fact that these damn embers need stoking and the wisps need fanning.

I focus on a dark pinch of ash near the edge. It ignites.

Joy.

Now to get these other cinders dancing. I look at a different section in need of a nudge. I stare for five or six seconds, then the same development—a new flower of combustion. I wish this was how camping worked all the time. I shift to a third spot and gaze intensely—it happens again. *Should I tell the wolves what's going on underneath? Would they even believe me?* Maybe right now they would, but even tonight the concept is almost utter nonsense. *You're right. This can't be. It is only in my mind, just a coincidence.* But, if this is an illusion, the flames are ecstatic for sure.

One more time for good measure. . . .

Yep. This is real. I'm controlling the fire. No sticks or leaves or breathing needed; it's all happening because of me.

I switch my focus to the main log, the big steady brute. There he sits, just basking there, showing off his inner source.

He reminds me of a pimiento cheese sandwich I used to eat. In fact—

He is the pimiento cheese sandwich I used to eat. His insides, the cheeses, ooze out of the flames, creaming down the ashes like lava. They root into the ground and use spider legs to shake hands with Jupiter's mound. This amalgam of mahogany and intensity now echoes and spews before me in this lovely, over-warming surrender. This shape-shifting entity called Jupiter spiders lava up my legs like little angels trying to find an angle to my mind, trying to show me . . . what we're both trying to find.

My jeans begin to breathe and speak like dragons do. They emit fiery letters that accentuate each word, with sparks flickering from their serifs, like the new age sheriffs working to dissolve the boundaries and the old tariffs of this world. At last, these sparks cut me deep and dry. They climb and climb, and now high in the sky I see all eyes, like a canvas of sighs that oblige my disguise that I've fought so long and so hard to size; they tell me that my capsize was not a surprise and the path I now fly is why I'm alive . . . and this night and this life and this ultimate firelight cry—all of it—brings wonderful peace to my side.

Electricity slides and glides around me like a winged cheetah, throwing its skin patterns on the tin lanterns, flinging black spots where my mossy thoughts have gone to die, and color where my fervor now lies.

And I am grateful. I am forever grateful.

Even good old Jeffrey is in on the action now—the spry fur ball—racing along the creek bank, with feet not visible, but indivisible from the grass. They hurry in a blur under his purple mass, heavy on Jupiter but supple enough to run past us into our future kindling, trying to become a tree, ever kindly, growing into the wooded scene.

Just then somebody in the forest puts on music, and the New Year's Eve noisemaker band strikes it up. As they hit each crescendo, each member of the band curls down to the ground only to uncoil and shoot up into the air like the party blowouts do. Fast curl-down, then they explode upright. Fast curl-down. Explosive upright. The forest greens and blacks transform the band into Tree Giants that lurk around my Armadillo Armor, trying to look for points of weakness, their huge stone-like bodies quaking and shattering my reality.

I have to get a grip and remember I'm on Jupiter.

There's a weight to these Giants—only increasing over the passing centuries' conquests and pitfalls—bumbling around in the forest, asking to penetrate the armor I once strongly held on to. Contrary Armadillo takes over little by little and my underbelly is now willingly exposed. They find a way into my circle and finger around in my body, caressing my arteries and blessing my blood with their brutal history until they reach my core, my anxious heart.

All kinds of ancestors now join the Giants around the campfire outskirts and, dressed in different garb from all time periods, look at me with blank countenances. There are Mayans, there are old French women, there are stumpy German boys, there are grasshopper people, there is a bishop mixed with a pharaoh. They are all different, but their faces pierce my soul with increasing levels of intensity. They drill down deep to my DNA, not to write or change, but to bring up to the surface what has always been there. They contemplate my dried-lava, spider-infested, dirty, starchild, peanut-butter-and-jelly-sandwich body and say not a word. And they don't have to, for I know why they took time out of their timeless paradise to interact with me around this fiery pimiento cheese. They want me to absorb my situation. Every time I turn my back on someone in need, every time I drink myself into a blackout or lie, every time I cut corners and make irresponsible decisions at work, every time I make a joke at someone's expense, every time I masturbate or play video games for hours on end, and every time I think about money over anything else, my ancestors are watching. They look through me without filters, seeing the long-view impressions we'll hopefully see one day, and they think about all the indignation and suffering they had to overcome simply to survive so that I could be here, right now.

I'm not sure when I became so hard on myself.

Once my ancestors are sure they've entrenched the message in my veins, they slowly dissolve into the forest, only to be replaced by images of my hunched over and consumed parents: My father—the rare mix of nerd and bodybuilder, white hair, his eyes distorted behind thick glasses, chest and throat perma-red from the oil-field sun. My mother—petite stature, fair cheeks dabbed with rose, short and curly hair, busy feet. The unexpected turn of events has me hovering above their study where they dedicate hours and hours to watching the news over hardwoods, dirty martinis, and wine. Just like the ancestors caressing me, headlines penetrate their lives and grip their veins like death. Drifting closer, I can smell the cheese and crackers Mom feeds me in the study whenever I visit during Thanksgiving and Christmas. I swear the food is right here, in my arm's reach.

Their faces, which are buried deep in their newspapers, don't acknowledge my prying, floating presence, but this is real. These are the holidays. I can taste the food and can hear the familiar James Earl Jones timbre of my father's voice when he clears his throat.

And then I realize I'm not the traveler here. They are. I'm pulling them toward me. No, something else is pulling them toward me. My reality and their reality begin to encroach on each other as the campsite atoms and molecules combine and exchange with those of the study. My consciousness of their consciousness also grows.

Then, something stirs them. My mom looks up. My dad looks up. Whatever it is, they swivel their heads toward me in unified alertness, skipping over every degree, like they've known my exact position the entire time. The two sets of eyes that have looked on me more than any other humans' now stare at me with piercing, one-step-ahead expressions. Never has their awareness of me been so affecting, and the small voice in my head goes a mile a minute because nothing about it sits well. My hands separate tufts of hair, making my scalp taut as I clench and worry. I squeeze my eyes shut, anything to stop pulling them toward me. I repeat the rational: *You are where you are. I am where I am. It's different.*

Before I resort to rocking myself, their molecules distort and get sucked into the waning blaze. And when the cooling campsite reappears, telepathy saturates every square foot when Antonio comes from the twigs and leaves near the cliff to reignite my world. *Thank you, my handsome Venezuelan.*

In the heat, all I need is Ava. There have been times when I've felt that I can't make it through life without her. My soul would be lost, helplessly knocking around in the deep space inside me. To me, she's like coming home from a long trip away, when the only thing you want to do is collapse in bed.

You take your shoes off, breathe deep, and just crash into comfort.

I wish I had a picture of her, even if she was behind sunglasses: her exhilarating, crisp brunette strands layered with pink, falling over them and down past her carnal lips. The picture would lead me to a dream, and my hand would lead the strands over the top of her ear and curve along the back of her neck to wrap her in my support and love. Our eyes would lock like birds of prey while phosphorescent colors streak across the black above, and the ground would bloom with fire-fuzz fruit when her lips nestle into mine. I never want to leave these moments with her. Time should know I need this, and stop ticking all the damn time.

The addiction factor has oddly scared me every so often. In those moments, I've thought it unusual that I don't want to do anything else but lie there with her, caressing her fertile thighs with my own. I want to always feel her hot breath skimming across my chest and never let go of her hand or let go of knowing she's looking up at me. The satisfaction of my incredible pickiness can be quite overwhelming.

And there she is, piece by piece, coming into shape beside me. Subtle veins give rise to the delicate tops of her feet, her plush lips, her olive thighs, and then, appearing as a glowing marble, her consciousness brings me to fear's doorstep again.

What's wrong with me?

I can't will her into my reality. I'm here and she's not. I can't be, nor do I want to be, in control of her. But she's forming before my eyes.

Ah! No, stop it. Don't think about her. Think about something else, anything. Think about the fire. Think about this real, physical thing happening in front of you. Mom, Dad. They're—

No. Don't do it. Please. Think about the spiders on the ground, all over me.

Fuck! Stop.

Think about the fire. Think about the pimiento cheese. Jeans. Brown and Green. Left. Right. Floating. Majestic.

"They're finally ready," Diego says. "Anybody want a hot dog? My skinny ass only needs one."

A hot dog. Something . . . not supposed to eat them. Think about the diet. Technically, not until Tuesday.

Hot dogs. Little pieces of animals wrapped up in penis-shaped tubes, then buns, and lubed up with yellow sauce?

Should have brought my own food. I want a hot dog. Open mouth. Do it.

Nothing. Can't talk.

Hot dog. Want.

"Here you go, dude." Diego offers me the extra dog.

Somehow food always brings me back a little. Before I can say thank you, the hot dog is down my throat. Welp. I guess my hand had no plans for me starting the diet this week. I'm not sure if I'm chewing on my cheeks or the hot dog, but it's damn good. The soggy bun, dog, tongue, teeth, and gums all blend together in a fruitcake-type snack that swishes around in my mouth and out of it so fast I'm almost out of breath. After my tongue checks for remnants of food, the permanent fixtures in my mouth go back to how they normally are. The nourishment has temporarily pulled me out of my fatigued head and drops me into my body again, but it's too short of a break for me to bring my heart back to square one. As the snack makes its way down my digestive tract, I head out, making my way through the stellar field, and find myself at the edge of the universe again.

At the edge, I need water. I always forget to bring some on long journeys like these, but I'm still so scared to leave the heat. There's lots of jobs for me, but getting up isn't one of them. My body can handle it, but I can't.

I remind myself I'm an armadillo. My body and mind are receptacles. I need water.

Please, fill me up.

"Here, dude. You want some?" Antonio says.

Impeccable. Thank you. You've done it again, my sweet, sweet prince.

I down the water, tricking myself into thinking of superhuman powers.

You did that. You made that happen.

Enough. No more of that. Get it out of here.

The farther you go into the woods, the longer it takes to come back. How much are you willing to risk? What if you can never bring back what you've found?

At the edge of the universe, I need not water. Layers begin to move through the night. Reality oozes and slides through itself. Ripples propagate through the fabric of the universe on the journey to my psyche; that which is dark—the invisible ocean of space—channels into me again, wave after wave. And space and time graciously back away, allowing this planet at the edge, my old house, my old friends, my parents, Ava, my ancestors, Machu Picchu, Hawaiian volcanoes, Spring Chicken, all to flood the camp.

There's no need for money anymore. I can just fly wherever I want. *No.* I mean, I can bring it to me. There's nothing to bridge to. I am already there. It all exists at this one point, and I just need to filter out all the other scenarios with my mind. I'm now wielding the true, all-encompassing power of the universe. *This is it. There is nothing outside of this. There is nothing else.*

And upon my shining horse rearing and neighing on the zenith, in my mastery of bliss, the entire mountain crumbles before me and I plummet to the valley floor. All possibility flows into my funnel, penetrating my Armadillo Armor. *This is dangerous . . . if it gets in the wrong hands. The evil, pain, and hate around. Power-hungry people could act in permanent, deleterious ways with this knowledge. The chaos, the abandon will consume all and earth with it.*

I drown into myself; my arms squeeze my chest and hug each other tightly. *Don't let go.* As I grasp, the fire dies down. I still can't speak. I want to get out of this hissing abyss of my head. I try to become more aware of the conversation around me. *Think about them, not me.*

"Not me," Diego says. "I like to think about myself in those situations."

What? What is Diego talking about? What are you talking about?

"What are you talking about?" Cyrus asks.

"If I was in your position, I'd think about myself," Diego answers. "You can't control what others do."

You can't control what others do. *Stop thinking that. This is just weird coincidence. What are you thinking?*

"What are you thinking?" Cyrus says. "That I need to be selfish?"

"You're putting words in my mouth," Diego replies.

Am I putting words in their mouths? *No, stop it. Just let go of it. Let's just move on.*

"Let's just move on, dude," Cyrus says.

Oh no. Stop. I am not controlling them. I am not controlling them. *What if I am?* How long will this last? Will this go on forever? *No, please. I can't handle this.* I want this to stop. *Get me out of this.* I want to go back. *Focus on your jeans. Your jeans are real—*

No, it's not working. There's no escape.

YOUR MOTHER AND I LOVE YOU

At some point in the midst of continental drift, my mother was born on the Mexican border, along a path of old territory battles southwest of the Alamo where the underside of Texas starts to slope down hard to the foot. Eleven years earlier, my father was conceived near the southeastern tip of Louisiana, just north of the cuttlefish's mouth as it flares out to the gulf, where, to this day, you can still see the imprint of racial tension on almost every street. And then he moved west and my mother moved east and they both wound up impressively close to the middle, in a city whose residents use petroleum to brush their teeth.

It was the tail end of a population boom created by a Middle Eastern embargo. My father worked with petrochemicals, my mother as a teacher, and once they settled down, they decided to add to the melting pot they lived in. They took a healthy portion of French, a bunch of Mexican, a pinch of

German, a dash of Spanish and Italian for spice, and then put it all in a stew to cook for nine months. When I came out, I was on track to be taller than most of my mom's family and darker than my dad's would have liked. They raised their only child as well as any parents could, and enrolled me in a small Catholic, Montessori school by the age of three.

Growing up in a Catholic family, I had heaven instilled in my mind, and ever since I remember remembering, I have feared eternity and all of the uneasy unknown it brings. I figured it would be a blast at first, being able to hang out with my uncle and grandparents again, maybe rattle off questions to kings and cowboys. I could brush my hands through the feathers of an angel's wings as we explored the vastness of heaven's reaches. Geographically speaking, I envisioned the stereotypical, white arching gates around an ethereal paradise, but my mind was young and dull, so that was pretty much it. No mythical beasts that spoke. No lush waterfalls that went sideways or upwards. No wind whipping the long hair of saints picking tremolos or triplets on screaming guitars in the background, and no veins of lightning forming from their acute headstocks, striking the air in bursts of fireworks and gobs of rainbow plasma. Just a bunch of people, standing around on clouds, conversing in robes. (Not talking inside of robes—that's ridiculous—but wearing them while talking to each other.) And then I thought, *Surely this would get old.* Of course, more people would die on earth and you'd get to meet new people over and over again, but if that were to go on for eternity, even that would get boring, right?

So I asked myself, *And then what?* Maybe, we could all organize fantastic new games to play. *And then what?* Maybe, we could learn to fly and be strong and acquire skills we didn't have time for when we were alive. *And then what?* Maybe, we could create new heavens to go to.

And then what? And then what? And then what? If your soul exists for eternity, there would be an infinite number of situations to go through, but I still saw it getting stale.

It was a preposterous thing for me to even try to wrap my head around—I know that now—but in prepubescence it led to many sleepless nights. I remember one in particular, when we'd come back from the park or some other public event where I'd probably smeared mustard all over myself eating hot dogs too fast, and something happened that triggered my brain into eternity mode; perhaps it was the start of daylight saving time, perhaps it was a friend saying he wanted to be happy forever. Whatever it was, it ended with an eight-year-old boy bawling for hours.

In my younger years, in times of weakness, my mother was the parent who took care of me, and being a stuttering child, I needed her frequently. Mama's boy was a term my friends would often use. The few times she couldn't solve problems I had (I could count them on one hand), she turned to the man in the background, the quiet provider, the constant business traveler, the man who came home from a three-month trip to a newborn son who didn't recognize him. My grandfather treated my dad like an employee, so as I got older, that was how my stoic father treated me. There were a few fun things we did together, like gin rummy and baseball, but we stopped the latter early on because my father's age (forty-six years older than me) was catching up to him. He continued to spend months out of the year traveling for work to Saudi Arabia, Venezuela, Singapore, Angola, and the point could be made that this was why I started doing poorly in school. One stirring night I came home with abysmal grades and my father then called me a basket case, which made me fearful of him and disappointed in myself but pushed me into being a hard worker ever since. I now understand that my father just didn't know how to express himself because his parents didn't make a huge effort. But the few times when his inner feelings did shine through were some of the most memorable of my life. His thought processes remain a bit of a mystery to me, but in those few times he opened up (whether he did it on his own or others made him) I saw the branch my apple fell from.

The night his eight-year-old son bawled his eyes out on the family couch, my mother talked to him in the master bedroom, eventually bringing him out to address me.

"Your mother tells me you're having a hard time. What's the matter, son?"

"I'm scared," I said. "I'm scared of heaven and living forever there."

My father picked me up, positioned himself on the couch, and propped me up on his lap—something he didn't do too much. "Well, that's only natural," he said. "Everybody is. I'm scared of it, too. I know it can be hard not to think about, but keep in mind that you have a long way to go, and there are lots of accomplishments waiting for you. Worrying about it won't do anything. You have your friends, your mother, your schoolwork, and you'll only need to figure it out when you get to it, not right now. I love you."

It gets foggy after this, because Dad customarily used Mom to help distance himself from me, so usually it came out "Your mother and I love you." Thus, on that couch, when he cut those first three words out, he eradicated all of my fears, and since it was so rare, my father's outward love also outweighed the effect of my mother's. The few times when she couldn't give enough, he reached down, found the dormant core hidden from even himself, and let me know that he was capable of nurturing emotions. I'm sure it was hard for him because I was no longer just a crying toddler. I was a child who could talk back, who could reflect how much he was helping me or not, and that's why it had such an effect on me. So even though I would sink into eternity mode sporadically over the next twenty years, I never again reached the tingling fear my eight-year-old self did.

Until now.

My father could have never predicted the onslaught of foundation testing that's presently happening to me. Tonight, I've reached those eight-year-old depths as well as my father's wisdom and plummeted past both. I'm in the deep, drowning in the gutter of the universe, and I'm deep alone.

SLEEP BAG

Look at your jeans. Your jeans are real. They look it, but the holes aren't doing what they're supposed to. The denim and my thigh flesh aren't separate textures or even concepts for that matter. The hairs have blended into the frayed cuts, as if my skin pattern is stitched into the jeans. There's sanity around here somewhere, I'm sure of it.

The fire will keep you going. The fire needs to keep going, else the cold comes in. Antonio goes to get more kindling, which seems like his thousandth time, while I'm left just wishing I could move my legs. But all we have to do is keep stoking it, keep feeding it, and we'll make it out alive.

This is where rationality is found. This will keep me from going down where the murky, dirt-bellies eat and die. But soon, Antonio and Diego will stop their jaunts of foraging, and it'll be my turn to bring more tinder to the thinning logs.

A voice tells me, *He who tends the fire can never stop. The fire is king. The fire is all there is.*

Late in the evening, infinity is unavoidably extrapolated from every thought I have, no matter how insignificant. *I see now.* Maybe this is what I was born to do: to tend to the fire, so that the cosmos may continue. My friends and loved ones will all enjoy the rest of their years, toasting and boasting, while I stay toiling at the blaze, in a small, closed-off world next to the universe, in the hidden third pocket that's long been forgotten. Everyone will stay lit in reality because of the great sacrifice of the fire-tender. I've been training for this changing of the guard since the womb, so if this is the path that was made for me, then I am ready.

No. I don't want this responsibility. I can't do it. Sure, I'll be fine for now, but in a few hundred years, my resolve will break down. And as my work fades, so will the universe.

The hearth glows like a faint beacon, off past marred and groaning jetties being pounded by waves, and my hands and feet are tired of aching, but nowhere near that of my brain. I'm done with this. Don't want any more. I wish the tent flap was already zipped tight, my body was already generating warmth in my sleeping bag, and I was a few hours deep in a dreamless sleep. I don't care for it—not any of it. This is too much responsibility.

As I try to get my body moving, I think of a horrible possibility: *Could it be that somewhere wires got crossed? Could it be that I'm crazy? What if my newfound freedom, my accepting of everything coming my way and the exacerbation of it, has brought me to the clutches of insanity? Maybe I've completely lost my footing in reality.*

I recap all of my actions thus far, the impossible visuals happening around me. *Maybe I've snapped. If I get the energy to go to my tent and get into my sleeping bag, am I really getting in my sleeping bag? When I zip up, does that mean I'm actually doing something else? Something unthinkable?* I've never felt such intensity from my thoughts before; I've never had these thoughts before. *Could my mind be using the sleeping bag to trick me, to act as some sort of construct to blind me from what is actually happening? If I were to go in my tent and sleep, would it be the Big Sleep? Would I never wake up?*

For the first time in my life, the jaws of suicide crush my entire being. The action consumes me. *This is it. This is where the curve bottoms out. This is where I see what I'm really made of.* Am I really capable of ending it all? I've never come close before. I'd like to think I love life as much as anyone I know. And then another terrible possibility: *What if this is all just the part where the big reveal happens? What if the transition was seamless and I've already done it? What is this feeling? I want this to end. I'll never go this deep again.*

The liberator of my mind has become the extinguisher.

I'm rendered useless, and no one here knows the truth of any of it. Do I speak out? Do I ask for help? If they knew where my mind has gone in the past half hour, they wouldn't be able to handle it, not right now. A part of me's glad my vocal cords won't help me. I must do this alone for the sake of my friends. They're not gonna share this burden, not today. I'm completely paralyzed, beaten down by possibility. I'm at the bottom of the barrel and there's not much left.

GIVE ME FUEL

Back to my jeans again. I try to focus on the separation of matter, and my leg hair sprouts through my jean holes.

My skin is not my jeans. My skin is not my jeans.

Ava used to tell our friends something similar about her army pants. I hold on to the reminder, because she's been here too. Years ago, she came clean to me while she was in the middle of her own episode, and I saw her go further down her grim path for months, withering away until she was a shell of her old self. It was one of those plodding stretches in which every day got tougher, longer, quieter. You wish you could just find that missing piece, that one antidote, because each day you didn't would get bleaker. Thankfully, I saw her slowly turn things around. Day after day, she stuck it through. We stuck it through.

It seems like every moment between us flashes on a high-speed train, an explosion of steel screeching and barreling through the gloom of the camp—each boxcar a different memory of the enigmatic connections we've had. The time with Fletch—a kid's toy, a stretch-monster centipede we took to music festivals, friends' houses, and weekend trips. Ava and I would each take one end and stretch him as far as possible, until you got antsy just looking at it. He was a tough, lanky guy, not reaching his limits until ten impossible feet. We would both be on our back legs, tugging away from each other, with him doing all the work in between. If you looked close enough, you could see his midsection losing shape, the green fibers pulling out from each other all spaghetti-like. No matter what was going on around us, we were only concerned with the elongation of rubber and the recognition in each other's eyes. At that point, Ava would try to pull just a little more, but I always had to stop it. And even though I tried to take care of him, Fletch eventually died a stretchy death, and we replaced him with Fletch II, promising to take better care of him.

But the first time I knew there was something special about Ava was during a celebration of sorts for my twenty-fifth birthday. Fifty or so yards from her front door, there was a trail we took that swung down to run along a creek that was just getting over the effects of one drought, but about to be devastated by another. Ava, Brown Sugar, and I were walking down by a handrail that two waist-deep, homeless people were propped up against. Among the tree roots entangled in a frenzy at the surface, their lips were locked while the man's hand was turning in circles around the woman's left breast, and as we got closer, he caught my eyes for an instant, then moved his hand down her side to her thigh while we passed. Their pelvises remained pressed together where the aboveground and underground worlds met. The water reflected their bodies, then the roots and trunks going all the way up, ending in two skies growing out of each other at the water point.

A little ways downstream, Brown Sugar and I squatted on stumps near the creek edge. River insects filled the sound spectrum as Brown Sugar and I turned to Ava who wore the mischievous grin she would later become known for, about to pull something out of her bag of tricks.

"Aha!" she yelped, punching her secret into the air.

Dangling and jingling in her hands was a belly dancing skirt I'd seen her wear a few times before. "Ha. Why would you bring that?" I said. "I don't get it."

"It's for the birthday boy."

I was still excited and hungry at my cubical job, not quite there emotionally. Under any other circumstances I never would have done it, but I felt a growing affinity for Ava so I put the skirt on and I owned it. I shook my butt and shook it fast—however awkward it was or wasn't—and my dancing on those once-submerged rocks was exactly what she was looking for. Ava's laughter brought her down to the gravel bed beneath her, but I continued on and she led me the entire way.

"Mmmmm, yeah, shake it," she said. "Shake it. Do it. Yes! This is exactly what needs to be happening right now. I can't believe it."

Ava tried to stand, but the rock bed left ashy spots down her arm. The small white marks on her tan skin left a natural cheetah pattern. I was still shaking when I caught her admiring her arm, and at once I knew what would happen next.

Do it, Ava. You know how good it'll feel.

She looked up at me with her sun-kissed eyes for what seemed to be minutes, and then she went for it. She rolled her entire body over the bed, making sure to cover every inch of her skin.

"Yessss, get that cheetah skin," Ava said. "It's good for you! Don't be jealous of it."

I wound down my shaky dance, and in that beautiful moment, I looked down at her rolling around in the bed, putting on her animal skin, and I knew she was the girl I had been waiting for all these years. We were somewhere beyond, running through the field of possibility, and in that fat spectrum we had found the same idea. Telepathy, the beta version.

It was approaching night when we made the trek back up to her house. We were trading dirty jokes, laughing under the greening woods, and there were two sets of clothes hung neat on the handrail over calm water, their owners nowhere to be seen. But as we took the final slant to her home, I had only one dominant thought that day, as there is only one now. And with it I've found my answer and salvation has come.

Ava said there were two things that kept her from giving up in her weakest times: the thought of putting her sister through that kind of situation, and me. She said she thought of me, the way I made her feel, my unconditional love. She held on to it, even if it was by the fingertips—a flicker in the unlit fields, a crystal shard in the depths. It was painful and long for both of us (my grief of course didn't hold a candle to hers), but she fully emerged like I knew she would. Even so, I wanted the turn to be because of her own strength, not because of outside forces.

Now I realize that my wishes were pointless and she was right. Because in thinking of her now, I couldn't go through with it either. I know I couldn't leave her with my mess. For this reason and for how much I love life, I can never. And now sitting here, camping with the moon-dogs, singing to our power ally, I see that those two reasons are one and the same:

I love life, because I love Ava. I love Ava, because I love life.

I didn't pull you out to fall in myself, to risk taking you back down with me. I did it so we could both remain on the surface.

Our minds play tricks on us when we give them a chance to speak. Maybe that's why we have hearts.

Thank you, Ava. Thank you so much.

One demon's been slain, but another awaits, wagging its heavy tail in my face. It's odd that my two biggest fears—eternity and death—have the potential to solve each other. *So what now? What are we going to do?*

The catalyst comes in the form of Antonio renewing the fire with an incident that occurred a few months ago. He's restless and moves around the circle, shaking his legs like a greyhound while firelight bounces off his long ears. He's excited about his fuel, and my insides leap for joy because I can finally focus on what others are saying.

Antonio and a couple friends visited a local spring that offers a downstream section where people can bring their pets, meaning there's always lots of dogs splashing after tennis balls, but there's one burly man, who most know, that bucks the trend and takes his boa. When he arrives, some people leave, most scatter, but some stand their ground, curious, watching every step he takes into the water with his forked-tongued, eight-foot long pet wrapped around his abdomen.

"Don't worry," the Tonkawa man always says, walking toward the middle of the spring, releasing the boa when he's waist deep. "She's trained very well."

Antonio says he and his friends were close to the man one day when the boa slipped clean from its owner to slither as it may. They had heard of the man and his pet, but one can only imagine what was going through their minds. *Ah, splendid! There's an eight-foot snake in the water now. I'm glad I can swim away fast. Oh, wait.* Being a curious man, Antonio talked with the owner about how he feeds his long friend, where he keeps her, how much she weighs, and if she's ever gotten hung up on trying to eat a pig or something too big for her jaws.

Never taking his eyes off his pet as he obliged the questions, the owner saw the boa make its way to Antonio's friend Lily. Her belly button peeked out just above the surface, her hands were skimming the water in circular fashion, and Lily turned from the snake just long enough for it to sneak up around her and brush the tips of her fingers.

Lily shoulder's shot up and she turned white while the friend she was talking to gave a high-pitched gasp. Paralyzed in fear, Lily watched as the snake slithered around her hands, flashed its tongue, and coiled around her arm and then her torso. The snake wasn't squeezing hard yet, but its owner waded toward Lily. After coiling a couple of times, the boa's head stopped in front of Lily's bare belly and moved back and forth a few inches away; its eyes focused on Lily's flat stomach while its body and tongue quieted.

"You're pregnant," the owner said, now right on top of them. "There's new life inside of you."

"What?!" Lily erupted. "Sir . . . please just . . . get it off me. I'm not pregnant. Just get him—just get him off me."

"I'm sorry, but you are."

Lily continued to deny it while the man took his pet by the neck and patted her on the head to uncoil. "I'm sorry if she scared you. Good luck in the coming months," the Tonkawa man said. The snake then curled around its owner and the two moved further up the banks.

"After the encounter, we left the spring," Antonio says. "The next day, I got a call from Lily. She didn't believe what the man said, but just to be safe she bought a pregnancy test on her way home. The man was right. The snake too."

"No way," Cyrus says.

"Damn. Them snakes be crazy," Diego says.

I can't believe it—the incident, but also that Antonio has brought me back, clearing my mind of the quagmire it was sinking in. I've come full circle; it's better when I step aside and get out of the way of the flow. *Step aside, man, release control, and listen to your wonderful friends.*

As soon as Antonio finishes, Cyrus describes the steps he went through during his ceremony with the Order of the Arrow, and I come back to a state of calmness. This is what I need. I need to hear others. I need to not feel alone. I need to know that my friends are going through similar or not similar things. I need to learn, but also be validated.

Diego picks up where Cyrus left off. As he talks, his chin starts to sprout hair, his bald head sprouts more, his cheeks become flabbier, and he begins to gray. *Is that?* . . . *Yes.*

It's George Lucas.

We're at the end of *Return of the Jedi*, in the forest with the Ewoks. Chewbacca's there. The deceased are there. The trees are alive with brotherhood, song, and celebratory dance. And I couldn't be happier. Elation, flutes, and furry beings are all that run through my mind, because something inside of me has been skewered and now turns and roasts on the pyre.

Antonio comes back from foraging and makes the fire grow, which reminds me to check. I think . . . I think I'm finally ready to help with the fire. It takes all my strength to get up and go for more branches, and though my legs and arms are stiff as nails, I don't feel chained anymore. Feeling bad that I haven't helped out yet (and because I don't want to get up again for a while), I set my sights on the biggest branches I can find. Beside the bluff at the base of the tree line, I spot one underneath a large pile of leaves and vines. Tugging at the branch a few times makes me realize it's matted hard to the ground. I put more stubborn force into the pull, but it only resists more. I give up for a moment to flex my hands and warm them with my breath, then go at it from another angle. This time the system starts inching up, the weight feels like I'm pulling up the entire bank. The vines around the branch take everything with them, but I manage to yank and pull out a ten- by four-foot section of dead bough and leaves.

"I thought I would make up for not getting some until now," I say, dragging the freed mat back to the fire.

"Ha ha. Dude! That'll keep the fire going for at least half an hour!" Diego says. "Good work."

As long as we keep telling stories, we'll add to the fire, we'll still keep spinning. I'm sure my pupils are in full dilation now, captured by the blaze. It's 10:00 p.m., and though it's not as intense as it was, I'm still not all back. The dirt's now firm beneath my feet, but even with the fire raging the damn temperature, that relentless bastard, drops again. There's only one thing left to do: I go to my tent to grab my sleeping bag. Before I do, I make damn well sure that I'm actually doing what I'm doing, not something else. I wrap the sleeping bag around me like a blanket and head back to the fire. Antonio, Diego, and Cyrus laugh at me, as I expected they would.

"Hey, that's fine with me," I say. "Go ahead. Freeze to death. That's fine."

"It's not even cold out here!" Diego says.

Before rejoining the group, I snag a hot dog and bun, splatter mustard all over the combo and my hand, and violently shove the food tube into my mouth. No idea why I'm so hungry. Unconsciously, I go for the big branch, wrangling a quarter of the beastly thing away from itself, and throw it on the rest of the kindled logs. The vine thorns take chunks of my fingerless gloves with them on the way to the embers, causing sparks and smoke to fly everywhere but especially in my face and down my throat. The fire rages hot, forcing me back in a crouch, my gloves disappearing into the flames.

Well, poop. *Sorry, little dudes. I'll be more careful.*

They say people born under Aries have a strong link with fire. With all the events that happened tonight, it rings true for sure. The sleeping bag slides down my shoulder and I realize I'm now in a predatory stance. My body has morphed into a jungle cat's, hunting the burning teepee. It has me. I yearn for envelopment. There's a comfort to the thought of existing in the heart of the inferno—the heat would run fast over my limbs and embrace me in the blanket of all blankets. I would breathe flames into my lungs, instigating a smoky dance that would char my insides, and my cells would shriek in pain, but I would be in love. I would no longer be carrying fire by hand, but by body. I could take on any environment in this reality or any other. I would never feel cold, the blistering flares my companions. I would never be alone.

Racing back into being, my fingers scratch dirt as I stop just short of jumping into the blaze. I push myself back and look around to see if the wolves have caught on to anything. They haven't—the blanket still covers most of me, hiding the craziness underneath.

Was I honestly about to jump into the fire? I guess it's not too surprising. I'm Searle in *Sunshine*, going down with the spaceship, reveling in my last few seconds, getting closer than any human being ever has, consumed by the power and majesty of the sun. In that futuristic, hypothetical universe, I could definitely see myself doing that—as long as I'd accomplished what I set out for.

The night runs on and everything comes back into focus. We move to drinking beer, and we laugh and commiserate until the early hours of the morning. Pretty soon it's just Diego and I, recounting all of our favorite movies, inventing ones of our own. After another hour, Diego says it's time for sleep. We dump water on the hearth and watch the embers hiss and cool inside the rocks.

I chug some much needed water, take my sleeping bag back to my tent, and check the time. It's 3:30 a.m. on earth; only nine and a half hours have passed since the start of the night's journey. Much like the encounter with Dr. Slice, I had no idea this would happen. How could I have? I don't know it yet, but tonight will set the tone for the most influential week I'll have ever seen.

Camping with the wolves ends on happy notes, but I'm unsure of myself. Not sure what to do. I don't know how to piece it all together or how I'll feel in the morning; but I do know something extraordinary has happened. Am I to go through with the ceremony in six days? The week diet is screwed, but the three-day diet remains uncompromised. I'm completely turned inside out, though. *Can I handle it or should I take a break? Should I tell others of the extremes I reached?*

Homer will know what to say. He'll help bring some sense to this. I need to go see Homer.

PART III: PROCESS FIT-UP PACKAGE

EXPONENTIAL FRAGILITY TOO

More than seventy dead. At least a thousand injured. Political tensions climaxed in a riot filled with rocks, Molotov cocktails, guns, and swords. Policemen looked on. Ambulances arrived late. Fans fell from bleachers to their deaths.

Port Said's Al-Masry beat Cairo's Al-Ahly 3–1 in a soccer game in Egypt.

I've just gotten back from camping and there's an update on this tragedy from a year ago. All I can do is stop reading. When someone says they're checking the news, they might as well say, "I'm catching up on the death tolls."

Soccer alone didn't cause this massive bloodshed, but the easy landslide into reactionary violence beckons for global focus. As we go about our days, satellites are fired out into orbit and fiber-optic submarine cables are run along every ocean floor, ensuring the shotgun-blast delivery of new power across our shores and down into our homes. And in the fattening slipstream of this fresh might, freedom drafts, waiting for the right conditions to be slingshot into the hands of any person.

I have no idea if I was harnessing any real power of the universe back at the campfire, but I did see a glimpse of what could happen. I saw the potential that we each hold and with it the same fragility.

I'm tired and stiff from the night on the dirt, and with the lingering effects of my dread and more drinks than was best, I've reached a depressing stew reading these tragic reminders. It's not even 2:00 p.m. and the day's already been brutal and restless, leaving me with inadequate focus for anything. I go to the fridge, open it, close it. I go outside, get the mail, start opening it, but end up tossing it on my dresser. I grab a fore arm strengthener, squeeze it a few times, just to throw it back on the shelf. Nothing does anything for me. Nothing is clear. The only thing that remotely makes sense to me right now is that I'm dirty—beyond dirty.

Undressing to shower, I find twenty or so bug bites on my pasty, chicken legs that instill in me the mantra: *you always gotta reapply*. I continue to scan the rest of my legs when I find a gruesome, red mess on the front of my left ankle. It looks like chunky tomato sauce in the worst possible way, and I turn my jean leg inside out to find the mess there also. I've had a bite like this before; it was from a spider and this one probably is, too. It doesn't hurt, but man does it itch. I won't give it what it wants, though, because I'm pretty sure that's when the pain will come.

I shower, staying away from scrubbing the spider bite and getting blood on the washcloth, but I make sure to run off all the red flakes of dead skin under a good rinse. I dry, primp, and grab a shirt I never take to my parent's house because I know Mom will do my laundry and ask questions about its one suggestive word. My foot misses the bottom part of my jeans a couple times because the knee hole has gotten so big, and afterword, I begin zipping up the fly when I remember the notebook.

The notebook!

The unbuttoned jeans slide down my wintery ass during the scamper to my backpack. I trip over them and myself, but milk it just long enough to stumble head-on into my camping gear. I get somewhat flustered, fidgeting with the shitty, shitty zipper that's halfway off its track. It opens only partially one way, then closes only partially the other, back and forth, until finally the backpack opens correctly. You're free, notebook. Feel your freedom.

It's open to the page I was word-vomiting on last night with handwriting that's barely legible, something like that of a six-year-old's. It reads:

Make it
Surrr
Totally surendring
to the fe, to the feeling
Let it happen
Total surrender to the moment
to life
Always

I read the chicken scratch over and over, and a piercing feeling overwhelms me. It's not quite déjà vu, more like having a dream about having déjà vu, where you've been told your future, and your future is the exact dream you're having. I stand in the threshold of my hallway, not knowing what my next move will be. I think, *This moment is big.* My knees become weak. I cry.

I feel helpless, scared, paralyzed. I can't call my parents—they wouldn't understand. But I need to do something. I need to just talk to someone.

I scroll through my phone to find Ava.

She answers but says it's a hurricane at the ER, so she can't really talk. Poor girl. She's always at the breaking point toward the end of her shifts. I do my best to be as curt as possible, and we make tentative plans on her day off.

Next is Homer. I hope I can see him. I'm never good at hiding anything, so right off the bat he knows something is wrong. I say I just need to talk about the trip, and he tells me to relax. I thank him for it. He's not busy tomorrow night, so we agree on me coming then to hammer it out. After we hang up, the silence isn't so deafening anymore. I'm still thoroughly blindsided by this whole thing, but the support of a close friend relieves me, if only by a small amount.

I'll sleep it off and see him tomorrow. Hopefully I'll get some answers there.

GRIP IT 'N' RIDE IT

Homer Phoenix is a lovable, buzzed blond with a baby face, deep sky blue eyes, one arm tattoo that has deep meaning, and one that doesn't. He attends school in a quaint town that straddles a river raging not with current but neon swimsuits, glow stick necklaces, and kegs floating in tubes. As such, his studies to prepare himself for a master's degree in Eastern, Western, and indigenous psychological and spiritual traditions appear rather eccentric. Then again, maybe not.

We try to visit each other every few weeks, engaging in six- to seven-hour discussions that usually begin with updates like a new foot ache, moving on to topics like one day we'll be able to walk through the Internet, and ending with an empty bottle of liquor that should not have been drained. Some of that is because of the long drive in between, but mostly it's because there's only acceptance, only freedom. Having a friend be a full gamut bounce board has been one of the most crucial elements over my course. Along the path from being a professional table looker-upper to what most people would call a "jobless bum," a select few friends have facilitated my change and supported my newfound curiosity, but Homer's the one who's been pushing my envelope hard.

I tell him that now, more than ever, I'm at a complete loss. I tell him every image and upchuck in my recent journey, even down to Jeffrey the fur ball. I make sure to put great focus on the grim places that I went to, bringing tears again. I'm such a big baby these days.

Homer gives me a much needed hug and we continue like therapist and patient. He tells me lots of people have gone through what I did, and it's only natural when one starts to head down these paths. He also reminds me I'm still fresh off a career change, and maybe I haven't let it affect me yet. Maybe I was just feeling the energy of repression. And finally:

"You cry because you're alive," Homer says.

Well put, my friend.

I inform him of my hesitation about participating in the ceremony in five days, which pinches at him a little, but he understands. He wants to share the first time with me, and I want to share it with him as well. The only way I could even consider going through with it is if he'll be by my side, ready to help me if necessary. And of course, he will.

We go in once more for a closing hug, and I clench him tighter, longer than normal.

"Can I ask you something? Are you reading into things too much? Are you getting caught up in it?" Homer knows me so well.

He gets up, grabs his chair from its back, places it in front of me, and says, "Tell me what you see."

"I see a chair."

"Right, but how do you know it's a chair?"

"I know it's a chair because humans made it for that purpose, to sit on."

"Forget everything you know about the chair. Forget the thousands of years of people using it to sit. Forget the different types and sizes. Forget the material. You know nothing about it now. Okay?"

"Okay. This is not a chair. I have no idea what this object is."

"But it's more than that," Homer continues. "Go further. If you flip it upside down and rest it on a table—or whatever this thing is—it's now become four long bracelet holders, right?" He takes it off the table and puts it in front of me again. "Or it can be used to throw at windows to break them. All criminals use these now." He grabs a pencil from his desk drawer and comes back to write a few marks on the side of the chair. "And see, now it's a journal. Is this starting to make sense?"

"There's any number of identities or possibilities," I say.

"So what is it?"

"It's anything I want it to be; it's everything."

"No, it's not. It's just a dumb wooden chair."

Shit, I was just starting to get it. But thinking it through, I know he's right.

And finally, he says the one thing that really butters my toast, the one thing that really tickles my pickle and sweetens my pie: "Trust that life is good and it will be. Everything's gonna work out, buddy!"

Thank you, Homer. You're damn right. That's what Spring Chicken always says. Deep in the forest, I lost my optimism. I lost my core mantra, the very thing that has made me who I am. What a great friend.

I was consumed with the negative and unknown phenomena that were going on around me, but I just had to take a minute to see that the universe has so much inherent good to find the peace I so desperately needed—even if it was temporary. I'll always be conscious of the bad, but I'll also revel in the idea that all will be well in the end. The light will burn on.

Laws are extruded for myriad quantitative characteristics, but there are no laws of beauty, no limits, yet the concept exists and persists just the same. That we can all qualitatively point it out or feel it to be present is, in itself, a miraculous notion. There is something about this that warms me, that makes me all the more excited about our evolution.

In the survival sense, beauty isn't necessary. The universe does not need a certain amount (that we know of) to go on, yet again, it's all so inherent. Does anyone look up at galaxies or nebulas with a disdainful face? The plethora of formations that have this quality only anchors my trust in a benevolent cosmos. (Unless one postulates the idea of beautiful evil . . . which is an entirely different discussion.)

Since the day I quit my job, scenarios have arisen that I never thought would cross my mind, and I'd be a dirty, dirty liar if I didn't say it's scared me shitless at times. But processing the situation with a friend helps so much, and it's also how I'll keep myself in check. That's how I'll hopefully evolve.

Even though I'm falling asleep, I say goodbye to Homer and make the late drive home. In the middle of the night, I dream that I'm in ultra-clean, white space, dressed in normal enough clothes, looking off somewhere that can't be seen. We pan back to reveal a huge brain beside me, which the dream elves or whoever supplies us with subliminal information in dreamland say is mine. A few moments later a saddle appears in my hands, and my brain doubles in size.

No matter what situation you're in, there's only one thing to do with a saddle: ride shit. So that's what I do. I throw the saddle on my brain, strap it down, swing my leg over and ride it like I used to gallop horses through the barrel races at Prude Ranch, which was, besides the house I grew up in, the first place I ever loved. I kick it for more than first place, more like it's my last ride; I'm done after this.

I wake up grabbing sheets, diagonal on the bed with a pillow between my legs.

I ponder the brain ride throughout the morning; it felt like I was onto something, but never quite got there. It's tough to make sense of it, tough to translate the full way through the filters into reality. The same goes for the details and for deciphering which ones to say goodbye to and which ones to keep in the hopes that they'll mean something later on down the road.

I surmise that the whole thing mirrors what Magnus did at the park. There's a group of us strolling through at two or three in the morning, and in the middle we lie down beside a large cluster of rock ledges on a verdant slope facing the tree line of our glassy, mid-city lake and out past that the lit-up yet emptied structures of downtown. None of us are up on the current phase, but after a few minutes the vibrant, orange moon, as full as can be, peeks out from behind the bridges, behind the corners of architecture, and in what seems a matter of seconds dominates the after-hours sky. Although the moon chooses to stay behind the clouds tonight, the refracted light, stretching millions of miles from the sun and bouncing off the dark satellite that's over 238,000 miles from us, is brighter than any of the buildings just a few football fields away.

Out to the southeast, beyond the row of eastside dives and past the cans and hot dog wrappings strewn about McKinney Falls, airplanes shove off from runways to roll and yaw in giant sweeping curves across the troposphere. They gain speed over to the west of the once-infesting Tawakoni spider webs and streak faster above the Colorado, the Pecos, and the Rio Grande, where the beavers topple trees to build homes that can span the length of the Hoover Dam. They touch down at LAX to refuel on the edge of urban sprawl, while a few minutes south ocean freight leaves port to pass by the Great Barrier Reef molded and layered by the secretion of coral. The drained freighters finish their long blue water haul by docking along the shores of Queensland, where termites build myriad mounds of mud taller than men. All are testaments to the amazing feats of the animal kingdom, and all are seen via launch at Cape Canaveral, leaving me to wonder what ever escapes being natural.

And as we turn, we all track the moon shooting up from the skyline like a white disc in molasses when Aurora says, "It's crazy to think that we're spinning like a—I don't know, like a Frisbee through space. How fast are we traveling?"

"It's somewhere around twenty-seven hundred miles per second," Magnus says.

"Wow, really?" Frigga asks.

"No, not really," he says. "I have no idea. Sounded good though, right?"

"See?" Frigga says. "Do you see what I deal with? I say dumb things to people all day because of this man. He's such a bullshitter."

All of us enjoy the husband-and-wife banter, and Frigga throws grass on Magnus's face, but always one step ahead, Magnus picks up more grass and throws it all over himself. He then pulls harder from the ground and brings clumps of dirt on his face, trying to lick at it like a baby that's covered in spittle and food. Frigga's semi-playful face becomes one of defeat, and you can see her thinking, *I just can't win with him.* Magnus continues to throw grass on himself but slows down, partly due to his awareness of everyone watching him, partly because the animal in him takes over for good. "Well, it's about time I take my shirt off," he deadpans. He then makes himself shirtless like a bear might take off a hat, just pawing at it, not really using his fingers.

Magnus is one of the most genuine guys I know. On the outside, he's a good ole southern boy, raised on a farm, in the deep elbow grease of his mom. He's a Lone Star man too—both the drink and the state. A couple years older than me, he also enjoys whiskey, wears boots most days of the week, calls potatoes "petaytuhs," and loves nothing more than working with his hands, doin' man shit. But he also loves playing with his psychotic cat, gardening, arts and crafts, and singing piano bar songs with me. One day, he'll send a picture of himself sitting alongside his laptop showing a random image of a monkey in the jungle and say, "Here's me and my three-month-old son. He's a dwarf, well, it's a monkey. This is in Equatorial Guinea. His name is Dodson, and he's a Libra."

He's an all-around hard-to-define man, which is probably why I keep him so close.

When our relationship first started at the engineering job, little did I know it would ever reach such heights. As our friendship grew stronger, we got to the point of having archaic conversations in their entirety. (Magnus's cat's name is "Sir Regal, Prince of Darkness.") These conversations would stem from cubical boredom or adventures in the country when Monday was days away. Long after I left, they continued over emails and texts and served as a way for me to check on the climate at the office, where I hoped Magnus was doing okay.

"This should bring joy to your heart," Magnus would say. "I have heard shouted oaths about eSlave all morn." (eSlave is documentation software.)

"My good sir," I'd reply. "With honor and respect, I appreciate the possible bringing of joy from your lips, but alas, it pangs me, for none should suffer that matrix of agony. It is a perilous journey with fruits for neither labor, patience, nor energy required. I shall pour out my goblet of the finest mead for the poor souls that suffer those imposed indignations with which I myself was once acquainted. May their unfortunate oaths be silenced with great haste."

"Fear not, honest and faithful companion. For your name doth not escape the lips on bitter tongue of any within these halls. Your memory holds fast with, and your vapors drift only with honor, among those few that remain."

"Such kind and moving words, Your Eminence, but it is of the indignation of eSlave itself that I doth speak, not the odors or blood I left in my cube of slow death. Be strong, my vigilant prince. Hold fast, for soon the day of your liberation will come. Your day shall shine on the faces of the world."

Later, I'll have a dream about Magnus giving birth to a triceratops (it's as messy as it sounds). Then I give him money to make more. He does. After the twenty-sixth one, we look around at seventy-eight brutal horns and turn to each other.

"Okay, that's probably enough." One room can only be asked to house so many horns.

Magnus made the hard times at work seem somewhat easy. It was a mighty crutch—especially toward the end—knowing I could go over to his cube and chill out for a few minutes when the stress got suffocating. We could say or do anything we wanted and the other guy would just nod, saying, "That's about right." It was therapy. As with Homer, I was so free to be myself with Magnus that I became a new person. Our relationship revealed to me the utter possibility of this world, however crazy it manifests; but not only that, there was utter possibility inside all of us—you just have to figure out what helps you access it. When I became an engineer, I thought it was the path I was to be on for the rest of my life. I just assumed there was nothing else for me. But in the interactions with Magnus, I found there were many paths, and it wasn't which was right or wrong anymore, but what you do with the path, on the path, that holds the weight. I'm glad he saw it too and put in his two weeks shortly after I did.

So imagine this man-child taking his shirt off in the middle of a park at 3:00 a.m., having just convinced all of us that the world is traveling at a speed he just made up. He's breathing heavy, emitting pheromones, lying down next to Frigga, half-naked and with his elbows on the ground. I'm nine or so feet from him, his upper body going up and down, articulately in the dark. His sharp intensity moves the grass in front of him.

You know that feeling when you know someone's looking at you? When you're looking in another direction, but you feel two beady eyes on you? Well, Magnus is looking at me dead-on, and I have that feeling anyway. His once vacant eyes become hyperaware. And this deranged creature, staring into my eyes like only those few people closest to you do or can, brings fear and familiarity simultaneously.

That stare. I'm caught in it. I can't turn away. He tilts his head ever so slightly to analyze me, figure me out. This thing, this animal—it's learning. His face becomes unglued, and his eyes now hold an expression that says, *I've lost control.* So let it be written. So let it be done.

His eyebrows rise as if he's about to surprise even himself. He coils back closer to Frigga and then throws himself into a barrel roll over the grass, turning over twice in my direction before ending up back on his elbows, inches away from my face. He's sweaty, brooding—a beast of the wild. His musk fills my nostrils. His body radiates heat and craziness, and his breath adds more of both. Our pupils catch each other's and widen.

"Sometimes . . . sometimes, you just gotta grip it 'n' ride it," he says with such authority I feel the earth moving beneath us. He digs hard into the ground—each hand grabbing a large tuft of grass—and jolts his arms like a bull rider. It's beautiful. Pure hilarity and truth.

It's Magnus being Magnus, riding the earth.

PIGGYTAILED BRIDGETTE

It's three nights before the ceremony, and I'm biting my nails faster than normal because the diet has already started and I still haven't decided if I'm going. It's also the night of Brown Sugar's show. He's a person and has a regular name, but he's decided that BS is what he wants everyone to call him. Fine.

We met at the age of thirteen. He had brown hair dyed with blond streaks, was already a lady's man, and had a knack for playfully arguing with our teachers, making him the first person to bend the borders of my conservative upbringing. We would stay close even after I left for a prep school in central Texas, even after I was dumb enough to double-major in engineering, and even after graduation when I sped away from Nittany Lion country as fast as I could to be reunited with the city I'll always love. I convinced Brown Sugar to move here and within a year we joined an Americana/Folk outfit called the Pentajams, which I would later quit mainly because of my job. But the joke's on that fucker, because I'd quit that, too, but before I did I met good ole Magnus.

Just months before I broke from the cubes, I took Magnus to see an Avant-pop band whose performances are so otherworldly they could charm a cactus into a dance. After my first time seeing them, there seemed to be all types of inspiration floating and meandering through the crowd, free for all to use, so I thought not to waste the opportunity and grabbed an idea out of the elation and high spirits to keep safe in the months that followed. The idea eventually birthed a character named Bridgette with long brown pigtails, sneakers, bracelets, an orange and purple dress. From there it developed into a children's book that she would later be the main character of, but due to life's curveballs, its treatment has since become a lower priority.

The show I brought Magnus to happened to be part of a larger circus-themed birthday party, which presented itself as a prime gathering for the misfits around town. He brought Frigga along and they went upstairs before the set to walk the line of burlesque accessory, deviant artist, and tarot card reading booths. Near the end of the displays, they found a tall man, dressed in gothic, Victorian attire, who greeted them by taking a hand to his hat to tilt the brim, on top of which were the petite old bones of a dog. Frigga and the man hit it right off when they found they both loved canines and the theatre, and she would later coordinate an event for him that she asked me to cover in a guest spot for a magazine.

I sent the piece in three months ago, cut my teeth on a few more articles since, and now have the chance to cover a late DJ show tonight that Brown Sugar also wants to go to. I find him at the first venue just before he goes on and tell him I'm sorry that I haven't made it to one of his gigs in a long while. Work used to be my valid excuse, but my soul isn't being Hoovered up anymore, so here I am.

The show goes great, aside from the fact that not drinking makes you a target:

"Hey dude, you want one?"

"No, thank you."

"Are you sure? They're free."

"I'm good. Thanks."

"Why not? You pregnant?"

"Yes. I'm pregnant."

Brown Sugar and I are out the door for the late show, but he's forgotten something inside, so we head back for a quick retrieval. I wait for him outside with Magnus, some other friends, and a couple of strangers who are still there, drinking, smoking, and laughing. I just wish I could partake. There's something to be said about being on the same level as others, but the damn diet takes precedence now. We're all gathered in an L shape partway down the loading ramp when a dude comes out, not looking or aware that anyone's there, and beats a mat full of dead skin and shit against the propped-open door. Millions of dust particles and mites are flung into the cigarette fog already riding the air and catch the exterior light and multiply, moving slowly over our group before falling slower over our faces.

"Ugh," I say, swatting everything I can. "There's so many. There's so many things around. I'm sorry, dude. Continue."

"Oh, don't worry, buddy," Magnus says, rustling dust out of my hair. "I don't ever have anything important to say. Ya okay? Ah, you'll be fine. They're good for ya. . . . Anyway. I mean, it's not like we were talking about the meaning of life or anything, right? All I said to them was 'I don't have cable or local channels.' My mom just looks at me, speechless. My dad asks, 'Well is it a problem with your landlord? They won't allow it?' I tried to make it clear again: 'No, Dad. It's a conscious, active decision on my part not to have any TV.' Then my mom looks at my dad with this dumbfounded expression, kind of like she's judging me. I know her looks."

"So Magnus," I say, still coughing a bit. "Familiar situation aside . . . what do you think the meaning of life is?"

"Well," he says, "naturally, the meaning of life is to get as many Southwest Airlines points as possible so we can go on a 'free' vacation that we already paid for through a magical reward system."

"That's the smartest thing I've ever heard," someone says.

An awkward silence follows light chuckles as my friends all turn to the stranger who butt in. "My name's Stu," he says, dragging off a cigarette, shaking my hand. Everyone trades their salutations and then separate conversations take shape.

"Yeah, definitely a nice, tight set," I say, a little on guard, avoiding eye contact. "Having a good night?"

"What do you do?" Stu asks.

"Whoa. You just go for it, don't you?"

"I suppose I do."

"Um. I used to be an engineer. Realized it wasn't for me— at least not right now. I've been working on drafts for a couple of screenplays. I don't know. I'm also just searching for what's all out there."

"Awesome, man," Stu says. "My hat's off to ya, making a change like that."

"I owe lots of it to support from my friends."

"So what else is filling your time up right now?"

"It seems like I've started fifty projects. There's a treatment for a children's book I'd like to work on again."

"Really? That's great. May I ask what it's about?"

When I tell him my idea, he's engaged, but between his flattering remarks it's hard to tell if he's hitting on me or not.

"Do you have an illustrator lined up?"

"No, I've been doing research, asking around. People say publishing houses frown when you try to bring illustrators with your projects."

"Well, I have a friend who is an illustrator and has been looking to get some work on the side. I understand what you're saying, but who knows? Would it be okay if I put you guys in contact?"

A little while later, Brown Sugar finds what he was looking for and we leave, but not before the chance encounter with Stu who had stepped outside for a five-minute smoke break. The best part is that after his completely selfless offering, he follows through on his word.

Not a day later, I get an e-mail from Stu's illustrator friend. She gives me her whole background, schooling, employment, a sense of her styles, and a link to a site with her art split out into categories. Over the next two days, we e-mail back and forth in a frenzy. We come up with some fresh ideas. We get excited.

And then something else happens: the illustrator sends me another batch of samples, and the last two sketches are of a little girl with brown pigtails, wearing sneakers, bracelets, and an orange dress—aside from the purple, a spitting image of the girl named Bridgette that has been running around in my head. I ask the illustrator if she's playing tricks on me. She isn't and says she had finished these sketches years ago.

I make a note to thank Brown Sugar for leaving his belonging at the venue and to thank the wolves for deciding the Armadillo medicine card would be read.

DADDY FRACTAL

So, the diet. They say for the ceremony to go smoothly you need to freshen up your insides, hang bouquets everywhere. I thought it wouldn't be hard to stock up on the grub I loved that I was also allowed to eat, but right now my nose has Kleenex scabs from the fight with cedar pollen, I'm hungrier than my first week of employment, and I would do foul and drastic things for some mac 'n' cheese. The bouquet diet is an eccentric, vigorous endeavor overflowing with envy, lust, and a hint of delirium. It's along the lines of veganism, I suppose, and my stomach isn't happy about it, not one bit. All day long he shouts: *Oy! What's going on up there?!*

No cheese, no vinegar, no vitamin C, no ice drinks, no pickled anything, no mustard, no grease, no meat, no decongestants, no alcohol, no sex, not even masturbation. In the more stringent ceremonies, all these—plus salt and many other omissions—are banned for a full month, rather than just the three days we're doing before and after. Because of the campfire with the wolves, my approach is by-the-book vigilance.

And we sit in silence, because I can't tell my parents any of this.

I've felt it coming on over the last few years, and I've now reached the point where I'm hesitant to talk about even the simplest topics with them. To my left, my dad has his head buried in his cheeseburger and potato skins. He doesn't look at me much anymore, and when he does, he looks above my eyes at my hair that's too long for his standards. To my right, my mom glares at the other end of the restaurant at a woman with a skull-and-wings tattoo across her chest. Mom says nothing, and doesn't have to. This type of conversing isn't sufficient, nor is the salad I'm shoveling down my gullet.

And so the rift grows.

My paternal grandfather had my father during the final blows of the Great Depression and raised him through World War II by frequenting the country club. My maternal grandfather would interrogate his daughters anytime they tried to leave the house, and usually prohibit them from doing so. It was only after he succumbed to abdominal cancer—leaving my grandmother no choice but to take on three jobs to feed five children—that my sixteen-year-old mother and her sisters were free to go to social events. And once she married my dad, Mom's racial background became a major source of disapproval for my father's mother, which eventually led her son—my uncle—to refer to her in names that won't be mentioned here.

Like many, my parents watched the United States grow up through the Cold War, Korea, the Civil Rights Movement,

Women's Lib, Vietnam, the Counterculture Revolution, and everything in between and since. They've lived through ample turmoil and animosity and boiled in pessimism and emotional frigidity for most of their lives.

When it's hard to communicate with my parents, when I can't find much compassion, no keeping the greater good in mind, I have to keep on telling myself that surroundings are powerful. They were also raised during a time when it was praiseworthy to march in line in the deep footprints of their parents. And with the Steve Pinkers of the world postulating a decline in violence, that we are presently living in the most peaceful time in human history, I can't help but feel that the pulse is changing, and my mind-set is different from theirs. I have to remember these circumstances, just as my children will have to do the same for me.

It took my older cousin's near-death experience to remind me, though, that there are still commonalities between us. I hadn't seen him in at least three years, but when my cousin almost died of food poisoning a while back, my parents and I made the trip to see him again, because death—or the chance thereof—oddly brings people together. Even though a project deadline was incessantly on my mind the entire weekend, the blue moon visit to my uncle's house that allowed me to converse with my cousin again was all I could have asked for. In addition, the weekend was one of the rare times I got to see my dad relax—he became happy, talkative, and engaged; no longer the silent provider.

When my recovering cousin and I were left alone for a few minutes, I took the opportunity to ask him if my uncle ever told him anecdotes of when our fathers were young. His encyclopedic brain was excited to impart information as always, and I was antsy to gain new insight into who my father was and is.

My father and his four younger siblings grew up moving from town to town around Cajun Country. The entire time my dad and my uncle were educated in Catholic parochial schools, but it was only after they had moved to Houston that Dad became disturbed by the bigger theological issues he learned about from the priests at his high school. He would read scripture to his younger brother at night, and after my uncle fell asleep my father would remain awake, reading more scripture and contemplating death, eternity, and the afterlife. On some occasions, he became overwhelmed enough to wake my uncle and discuss his fears throughout the night. Even though he was the younger one, my uncle would try to corral my father's thoughts, but how could he console such a stoic person?

When they moved from Texas back to Louisiana, my dad encountered a Jesuit principal who helped him begin to address most of his troubles. As Dad grew older, he would sometimes joke that he and his brother still had the "cursed Jesuit strain" from James Joyce's *Ulysses*, but between waking his brother and talking to his crying son on his lap, my father had learned how to cope with his own mind. He developed a strength, which he would try to pass on to me.

It might sound insensitive, but I've drawn a lot of peace from my father's long ago sleepless nights. There's something about going through the same pain or hardship as someone else that makes you feel not quite as screwed.

But how do I tell my parents of my most recent bout? Do I even need to? I sit in wait, eating dressing-less salad, with no clear approach to ending the silence. My mom finally breaks the spell by asking why I'm not eating meat. Ugh. I can't even tell her why—that's how bad it's gotten. She then leans in to whisper, as if she was going to tell a dirty secret. "You aren't becoming—God forbid—a vegetarian, are you?" she asks, only half-joking.

I should be able to answer her straight. It's just another aspect of my life that I lie about or keep silent, another suit like the one I wore for work. How has it gotten this out of hand?

We get the check, and they drop me off, but not before they ask what I plan to do monetarily in the future.

"I'm handling it," I say.

"Are you getting more projects through the production company?" Dad asks.

"I just started, so it's been slow."

"When did you quit again?" Mom asks. "Has it been five months? How are you keeping up with rent?"

"I still have savings left. Been working for a friend here and there. Don't worry. I'll figure it out."

"Well, maybe it's time for you to ask your old colleagues who moved on if you can work for or with them," Dad says.

"I'm sorry, Dad. I can't do that."

"Well, just don't withdraw from your 401(k), whatever you do," he says.

"Thanks, Dad. You guys have a safe trip."

They drive back home to Houston with full bellies and no change in their relationship with their son. I'm left drowning in my own dilemma, and still hungry because the salad I ate wouldn't satisfy a child.

In my room I stare at the ceiling for twenty minutes, day-dreaming about everything I've never told my parents but plan to, someday. "Behold!" I would say, after jumping from a speeding train into the middle of a field where my parents are waiting for some reason. They would observe the fervor in my eyes and the will in my stance, and although nothing concrete would have changed, that's all they would need. The mask would fall and they would know everything. No longer seeing their quiet and innocent boy, they would know me for the first time, know what I've become and how far back the change was. And then the wind would kick up as I said, "You helped make the man who now stands before you. And I am sorry."

It's two days before the ceremony, and I've bought sage to cleanse myself and my house after conferring with Carmela about what went on under the cypresses, about the sleeping bag and the pimiento cheese. Holding the bundle of New Mexico sage in my hands, I wonder if I'm just doing this because I was told to, or do I feel it, do I truly believe? Is this necessary, this cultural appropriation wrapped in plastic and purple twine? Will I let my hesitancy overpower the situation? Did I really slip up and eat pizza last night?

Holding this sage in my hands, I realize I've never concentrated so hard on lighting something on fire. It all has to be crystal clear: I'm not just cleaning my slate, I'm putting a coat of wax on it, too. The brush burns, and as I take it to the jambs and the threshold of my door, the smoky eddies carry atoms around, covering up the old, bringing new smells and hopefully new hope to the forefront. Maybe this is just an easier way to put focus on something. Maybe the only thing that really matters is the intention in my mind.

I sage every crevice and gateway, moving like a figure skater with the Olympic torch, extending all the way up to the nooks and all the way down to the crannies. After the house, I turn around counterclockwise in place a few times, saging myself, letting positivity come and the oogie-boogies go.

I've cleared my schedule for the next day and a half, but lucky for me, I still don't have a full-time job so there isn't much to clear. It's not essential, but it's recommended to be in a relaxed state of mind: "Avoid any upsetting circumstances. Make sure to get proper sleep. Don't do any strenuous activities. Don't watch violent TV or movies, and be selective about what news you watch or read." So I've been giving myself a healthy dose of comedy talk shows, soothing music, and reading. But after too many hours of being inside, I'm ecstatic to hang out with Ava.

I pick her up with a sack of surprises in my backseat, and we drive to one of her favorite places—a public art installation in the form of a picnic table, on a knoll nearby our mid-city lake. Out of the car, I follow Ava underneath two white, tree-like chandeliers and down the perhaps thirty-foot long aluminum table. While she takes her seat, I set the bag down on the painted metal top that's etched like decorative table cloth and lay two lighters and two white poster boards beside it. I turn to Ava.

"Well, what are you waiting for? Start making art."

"Um. Whaaat?"

"I kid, I kid."

From the sack, I take out the four differently colored candles I got the night I spoke to Homer. Paying homage to his river town, I had settled for neon pink, neon aqua, neon purple, and black.

"Nice," Ava says. "I've always wanted to try these out."

"The first second I saw these, I thought of you. It's been a while since we made art together."

"Aw, I'm so glad you wanted to. Awesome color choices, too! You're the best."

Neither of us have done this before and have no real plan, so we each pick our candle and light it over the boards. The melted wax trickles down on the white canvases, and we go about moving the candles in every shape and direction we see fit. Slowly a pattern emerges, and our droplet method becomes one of color balance, so we switch candles to keep an even spread.

"Huh," I say, standing on top of the table. "We made sort of a fractal pattern. You know about fractals right?"

"A fragdole? I don't think so."

"Ha. It's anything that has a self-similar pattern. . . . That tree over there. You see how the branches come out of the trunk, then smaller branches come out of those branches, then again, then leaves sprout from those smaller branches. And even inside the leaves, the veins that transport the water and nutrients. There's one main vein down the middle, then smaller veins branching off, and even smaller veins off those, mirroring the tree as a whole."

"That's neat. I never knew. Fragdole."

"Yep. And it's fractal. C, T, A, L."

"Oh. Nooo, I think it's fragdole. Pretty sure of it," Ava says, working me into a grin.

I make the choice not to tell Ava about my weekend yet. I'm going on a hunch that I'll make more sense of it and have more to tell her after tomorrow. We cover almost every inch of poster board with wax droplets, but have to stop because the candles now look like sad, dead globs, and our thumbs are burnt and bruised from striking the lighters so often.

An hour or so later, I drop her off, and since my energy has been renewed, I decide to go back to the lake for a light jog (hoping it won't agitate too much) on its perimeter trail. Midway through my runs, I always stop for water at the same fountain, next to a wall where I once graffitied my love for Ava. It was eventually painted over gray a year and a half ago but is now the backdrop for a huge, circular flower garden. Today, though, I'm mesmerized by the fractal phenomenon at the bottom of the fountain bowl. I can't believe I've never noticed how the water pools here, because as above, and so below, fractal behavior is everywhere: galaxies, nerve networks, seashells, lightning, broccoli, peacocks, pineapples, clouds, mountain ranges, shorelines, the feeling I get when I eat an entire carton of Cool Mint Oreos, the uncanny miracle of the human body. Our lungs, brains, and circulatory systems all exhibit fractal qualities. Even so, it's a huge revelation for me.

Slurping water and looking down into the bowl, I think of how I'm imitating my father. If human generations are used as the scale, the pattern begins to emerge: some little remnant or structure of my dad's psyche made it into my mother's womb, where it was nurtured and would later become a part of his baby boy's psyche. And it now lies in wait inside of me and could make it into a womb that will one day contain my offspring.

This eternity remnant first reared its head in grade school, when a teacher claimed she could make us walk in one direction toward the back wall of the classroom for the rest of the period without us ever reaching it. I don't remember what prompted the lesson, but it began with my teacher making us stand ten feet from the wall, awaiting her commands. We lined up with our Teenage Mutant Ninja Turtle shirts and light-up sneakers, and then she told us to walk halfway. We confidently marched to our best guess of where that was, and she told us to walk half the distance again. And again. And again. I imagine on that day my face was probably covered with dried peanut butter—remnants from the sandwich my mommy made for me that morning—but the peculiarity was happening behind the peanut butter, inside my brain, when I found myself inches from the wall. Heeding the command soon proved difficult for everyone, because our clunky shoes wouldn't let us advance much further. Eventually we looked down at our feet in defeat, because our motions weren't articulate enough to continue the lesson.

But in reality, the lesson was already over.

Since then, I've ridden the sea with eternity: just when I've started to be calm and feel good about it, I've gotten pulled from off my feet and lost my orientation. But the possibility of my potential offspring experiencing the same fears plants a seed in me to overcome this anxiety. If my facing it head-on helps me gain the tools I need to help my child's disposition when manifested, then I am going to do everything in my power to ensure that happens.

I've decided that I'll actively search for a remedy for this open wound in my bloodline. Having had time to process the campfire, it's hit me all at once: recording experiences is the kindling to my advancement. Without that, there would be no connection to the past, nothing to pass from generation to generation. Tragedy teaches us how to live better. That's what it's for.

I have chosen to go through with the ceremony. I want to prepare for my child or children. All that I endure and conquer now will further bolster my ability to provide them what they will need. And I'll have my friends there with me.

PART IV: TETRAHEDRAL JUNGLE VIXEN

ONION CLEANSING

Homer Phoenix bangs incessantly on his new drum, his huge pot filled to the brim with kale works on the stove, Brown Sugar and I bubble over loudly with excitement, and my poor roommate is knee-deep in emails and conference calls. I'm sorry, girl, our heads are somewhere else, but we'll all be out of here soon, for today is the day the three of us have been talking about for months.

I rush around getting my backpack and everything else ready before we have to leave for Carmela's, and aside from the jiggling of the butterball sack above my waist, I'm feeling kind of astronaut-y. It could be because I'm a little lighter than usual from fasting all day, or it could be my anxiousness over the chasm I'm about to explore; either way, missing two meals won't stop me from being sharp and animated about such an anticipated night. I've only heard a few snippets of Carmela's experiences, so I'm not sure how it'll go down, but

I can't stop thinking how tonight could alter perspective for me. And that I need to eat ten Snickers bars right now.

What did you say? Where are they? Give them to me!

Arriving at Carmela's manor reminds me of driving up to my prom date's house: Can I still back out? What am I getting myself into? Going all the way is kind of scary. Will my parents approve? I hope there's cake. An older woman with a white parrot on her shoulder greets us under the columns of her massive door. I give her a big hug, swatting the parrot feathers out of my face, and introduce Carmela's mother to Phoenix and Brown Sugar.

"*Como estan*, boys!" Luna yells.

My friends' faces turn bright as they greet this exuberant but small lady while her parrot yells, "*Awwwwk. Helloonw.*"

"Please come in. Carmela will be down in a second, and the tea is almost ready."

"*Tea. Gotta some tea,*" the parrot squawks.

The room we're led into isn't so much a living room as it is a living hall, and Carmela comes hopping down the long-ass, oak staircase as we're dumping all of our luggage into their multiculturally decorated space. I squeeze her good, and in her ear, say that I am forever in debt to Luna and her for giving us this opportunity. Carmela is a Chilean-Peruvian girl, one of those angels that you wish you spent more time with, but haven't given as much love to as you would like or as she deserves. I don't know why, maybe because life gets dumb like that sometimes, but even so, she remains as loyal as ever and brightens up your day every single time you see her.

"*Awwwwk,*" squawks the parrot.

Luna comes back with tea and a box, sits down, and tells us how the ceremony affected her life. After many years of long days, she had molded herself into a tenacious business-woman who'd always been on the offensive, but after taking over a construction company she found herself consumed by her work, ever agitated, and making decisions she wouldn't normally make. Her first ceremony brimmed with grief and forced her to take a step back. It was the push she needed to understand that she had to renew the bond with her children and develop a more sacred approach to her business.

Between my junior and senior year of college, my friends and I did what all newly twenty-one-year-olds do and sought out all the beer specials around and guzzled them down, using the last of the paltry money we had saved. I remember the summer well, because for all intents and purposes it was the first time I felt like an adult. Of course by early June, my employment search was quickly unraveling into a major shit bucket, so much so that telemarketing gigs and sperm banks were beginning to look attractive. I had been a line cook the two previous summers and didn't want to work with food again, but eventually I bit the bullet and found myself heading for an opening in the kitchen at a strip club down by the airport. I was nervous for what I might find at The Landing Strip, but luckily I was only halfway there when a friend of mine called and said he had gotten three of us jobs with Luna's construction company. We all celebrated that night, though a part of me regretted that I wouldn't get to see the raw truth behind the velvet curtains.

Luna added hundreds of jobs to the community by buying rundown houses and small commercial complexes to fix them up and rent them out gentrification-free—quite a large task and just one successful arm of her mini-empire. We worked under the supervision of a jovial, high-pitched, bowling ball-shaped man named El Pintor (which is Spanish for, simply, "The Painter") and, within a few weeks, were pretty comfortable with our responsibilities of helping him paint, hanging insulation, finding hidden corners to sleep off the previous night's booze, and other random jobs. After we got our feet wet, he took us to a house in the final stages of construction, where he wanted us to apply the first exterior coats. Later that morning, he got called to an emergency job and told us that this guy Jorge was the supervisor we were to work alongside for the rest of the day.

Jorge was a quiet man, though he acted above us when the lack of our handyman knowledge—that he felt any normal man should have—became apparent. There was some validity to his behavior, but I figured it was more due to the fact that we were three gringos (two of us were exceptionally gringo) because all I saw was disappointment in his face when he first spoke to me in Spanish and I told him that I didn't speak it. (When I was young, I told my mother to stop speaking to me in Spanish because kids at school were making fun of me, and since then, I've let a lot of people down.)

The next day, we were back with El Pintor, and he asked us how it went with Jorge.

"Just fine. Why do you ask?"

He thought to himself for a few moments, then decided to tell us in his steaming tea kettle voice: "That guy Jorge. He's a bad du'. He was at a cantina. You know, *tomando cervezas. Mas y Mas.* He was all *borracho* and started fighting about *política* back home with *dees muchacho. Un muchacho grandísimo, verdad? Me entiendes?* They yell and shout, *y chingara grande* punche him in *la boca!* In ees mouth. Johnny gets knocked down and *el pinche muchacho* jumpe on eem and starte beating de fuck out of eem.

"Jorge came from *trabajo y* remembered he had a blade in his jeans."

"What?" one of my friends asked. "A blade?"

"You know, like a blade . . . *como se dice?*" He pulled one out of his jeans and showed us.

"Ohhh, a box cutter," I said.

"Ah, *exactamente. Sí, Sí.* Bo' cuttas. *Sí.* He take de ting out of his jeans and cut the *muchacho* face. The *muchacho* fell back, but then jumpe on eem again. And then Jorge jus' estarte cutting. He ju' keep cutting and cutting and cutting. His *hombres* try to stop eem, but he jus' keep cutting and cutting. And he kill the *muchacho. Lo mató.*"

We looked at each other and then at him to see if this was all an elaborate joke just to scare us—in a few seconds he'd burst out laughing and say, "Gringos believe anything!" But that didn't happen. El Pintor was dead serious.

The three of us had never been around something so raw before, and we were to be up close with it off and on for the next two months. Between coats of paint I would watch Jorge just to absorb how a man extinguisher moves and behaves. How close was he from the edge as his days went by? Was there anything that would push him to snap? I would continue to ask these questions to myself and my friends, but over time Jorge became just a normal man who went about his work like any of us would.

No illicit behavior came that summer, and as far as I know, nothing has since. After that one night and the record strike it came with, he could have been rejected again and

137

again, he could have gotten desperate enough, he could have spiraled down, but Luna's heart intervened, possibly saving one life or more in the process.

Luna takes out a bundle of sepia- and umber-colored feathers from the box, explaining they're from an owl who oversees her land. When the bird first came to the property she was scared, thinking it was a bad omen, but when she realized that things—in fact, all the things—were happening in her favor, the owl came to be a protector in her eyes. She then made him a little black box and hung it on a branch forty feet in the air for him to rain protection down on all her sacred land.

"*Awwwwk*."

She motions to the empty part of the couch next to me. *What?*

"Do you see?"

She motions again, this time with both of her hands and a stern nod.

"You want me to lie down?" I ask.

"*Sí, sientate*. Here."

I take off my shoes and position myself.

"No!" she yells, hitting me. "Do not cross your legs."

Ugh, but it's so uncomfortable with these splayfeet. "Oh, okay, sorry."

As she moves above me with the owl feathers, asking me to close my lids, I lie there thinking of my parents and all the client suits I've interacted with in the past and how they would roll their eyes at this scene. Luna fans and whips the air over my body with the feathers spread out while she whispers words I don't know, and then I realize tomatoes are acidic.

And the damn pizza. A little pinch of bummer from not following the diet to a tee sets in, but I'm still fairly confident in a rewarding evening after the two sage cleansings and these feathers on top. The necessary separation from last weekend is becoming more tangible by the second.

"Okay. You are done," Luna says as she taps my forehead with a feather end. "Did you feel it?"

"*Awwwwk!*"

"I felt waves of energy," I semi-lie. I didn't feel too much, just wind over my body.

I watch Carmela, Phoenix, and Brown Sugar get cleansed after me as this calming afternoon takes over, and before I know it, we're cramming our potlucks, sleeping bags, pillows, purging bowls, and seven bodies into a Suburban. On the way to the ceremony, I look out the window at a city that's about to finish its workweek, partially because I want to take one last snapshot, partially because my body is contorted in the back-seat and facing the other way I'll be Eskimo-kissing Phoenix.

After the long drive, a few wrong turns, and accidentally trespassing on someone's property, we arrive at the ranch that holds the ceremony grounds, and I jump out to resuscitate my legs as car after car pulls up and empties out adults of all ages. Elements of nostalgia and regret circle down on these grounds, but the predominant feeling of watching a sixty-year-old man unloading his pillow and sleeping bag from his van is happiness. Happiness because getting older doesn't mean you have to stop adventuring.

In the main ceremony space, people of all walks of life greet us as we pick and prepare the spots we'll be in for the next eighteen or so hours. You can tell which people have done this before, with their plush comforters and their hand-made musical instruments from which intricate tassels hang and beads dangle, and there are the people who embody this every day, with their entire wardrobe and overall presence dedicated to the ceremonial aesthetic. And rounding it out, you can tell which people are the first-timers: we're calm on the outside, but under the surface we're buzzing at breakneck speed.

I think of where I was ten years ago: a quiet kid who had dreams of playing baseball for as long as he could. I think of where I was five years ago: rushing home from my job so I could get online and repeatedly lose games to racist thirteen-year-olds. I think of where I was two years ago: slightly still Catholic, slightly going cubical crazy. And I think of where I was last year, having never thought of any of this, but still, somewhere deep down, it's always been there.

Luna says goodbye, but before she leaves, bless her heart, she hands all of us decorated cloth, each piece with complex patterns woven into the fabric by the Shipibo tribe of Peru. Carmela's used to her mother's generosity, but the three of us are beside ourselves and each pick the one we like. The cloth that has purple draws me, and when I flip it over I'm set on it, because each one is made to be a song for the protection of some facet of life and mine reads, "Song for the Protection of Children." I rub the writing with my fingers and place the song on the altar at the center of the ceremonial circle.

And as we rest in silence on our knees, preparing for the inward journey, the sun casts a single flat sheet that stretches from a southwest window toward Phoenix and me for Eagle and Snake to walk through. They're normal-looking people: he could easily pass for a banker or construction foreman, she for a lawyer or an airline pilot. Either way, I'm excited for Snake's rainbow woven shoes, for Eagle's genuine demeanor, and despite my intense experience a week ago, I also draw comfort in knowing that three great friends are with me, ready to hold hands and plunge into these foreign waters.

My potbelly is also doing surprisingly well.

A bell rings and middle-aged white men, older South Americans, thirty-somethings with fuchsia hair, ranch hands, a wife and husband, a mother and daughter visiting with each other all part and go to their individual places for the evening while I meet eyes with Phoenix and say, "Here we go." Once it quiets down, Eagle outlines the structure of the ceremony and stresses community when he sees one man and his sleeping bag sitting outside of the circle. He urges him to come in and gets some opposition from the man, but Eagle's gentle persistence helps persuade him to join the rest of us and scoot along the floor.

He lays out ground rules, necessary pieces of information like the candlelit path to the bathroom and what to do if you find yourself in trouble, and tells us the order of the segments throughout the evening. The last step before taking the cup, he says, is to go through a tobacco ritual, where every participant must be blessed and blown with smoke as a symbol for initiation and cleansing. This is meant to further bolster the walls of all of our inner castles. Snake reveals a jug that holds the sacred, dark brown concoction, and down the circle, one by one, people go to kneel before her. She asks and checks the name, then swings a pendulum above the jug for reasons I don't quite know, but an old woman named Bear gets a full cup while I get a half, so maybe that has something to do with it.

We are now told to receive the dark creature, to bring her close to our hearts and introduce ourselves, and only then may we whisper our intentions into the Dixie cup she resides in.

"Hello. Hello, you potent thing . . ."

It's not nervousness that trembles the nectar in front of me, just a completely foreign feeling, like I'm not even kneeling in this space. But knowing the good chance that Phoenix will go on to study these practices for years to come, this night seems all the more necessary. Beside me, he clutches her in his bosom with reverence and peace, and I take a hand to his shoulder.

"May this be the beginning of a long journey for you, my friend." He looks back to me with heartfelt eyes, and for a second, I think he could cry.

"Thanks, man. I'll see you soon."

Eagle tells us all it's time to drink, but the brown essence can curdle if the drinker is timid, so do so quickly. We're now eight or nine hours into our fast, and because she's known to be a jealous teacher, once we drink her we can't let anything else in, not even water.

Everyone in the circle begins to drink and some have a harder time than others. She's a vile, viscous creature, leaving people straining, gagging, and dry-heaving, while she works her way down. I just go for it and shoot her, so she's bad but not too bad in my mouth; the aftertaste is earthy as hell, but more tolerable than other drinks I've thrown back. Eagle says swishing water is allowed, but as said before, no swallowing. People do so, but there's still a lot of grimacing going around, because for the timid, I imagine it's more like drinking sand as you make your way toward the bottom. Eagle says we must try our best to not throw her up, either—at least not for the first forty-five minutes—because she loves the waiting game and you have to play it her way until she's ready to clock in to work and punch your clock.

Eagle turns the lights off, immersing us in blackness, and as the eyes adjust, moonlight creeps in on this tender, manicured space that rests in the middle of this crazy country of ours. Eagle begins to lead us in visualizing sacred shapes—one octahedron descending from above, another ascending from below—surrounding and protecting the circle from the unwanted. This is the final layer of protection I need. This is what will keep me flying in Peter Pan Land.

PINWHEEL LAND

"Spirit of the East, we welcome you," Eagle says, beginning the quest portion of the evening. "We invite you to initiate our thinking. We look to you to show us the clarity of vision and emergence of form. Thinking must always precede doing. When the sun comes up, we look to the East."

This place, and many others like it, was built for one purpose: to host ceremonies like this. People rustle around and get comfortable with the feeling of the blanket of anticipation inside these walls. That and the human breathing. Deep, conscious breaths, as if some of us are learning to breathe for the first time.

I don't notice anything for the first twenty minutes, which leaves me wondering if I slipped up in the diet more times than I thought. All of a sudden, Phoenix's breathing picks up and ghost fingers run down my spine. At first it seems like he's trying to calm himself down, but then it's more like he's in labor, then louder as he tries to suckle up every molecule in the room. Now I hear Carmela join him and their breathing amplifies my nerves, but I don't realize until a few moments later when my stomach starts to turn that it's really her.

Don't puke. Don't you even think about it.

Even though I can't see, I know my purge bowl is at the foot of my sleeping bag, so I lie on my stomach as a last resort and zigzag my wobbling hand until I knock it.

It's cold too. I know, I know. I'm an incredible wuss in this weather.

The battle in my stomach grows violent, forcing me to grab my pillow. There's something about the tight-to-the-chest grasping that takes me back to my childhood, back to a small French doll that I used to sleep with as a boy. He had a long, floppy blue hat stitched to his head and clown clothes that fell off at the shoulders. But he was no clown. Still isn't, I suppose. He's stayed with me all these years, too—he's in a bag in my closet, probably thinking he's better than Spring Chicken.

I feel it drop again. *I'm gonna have to bring thermal blankets next time so I don't worry about temperature.* Phoenix seems to be fully under the power now, and I just hope the transition is smooth for Brown Sugar and Carmela. I also remind myself that if anything goes wrong I just need to find something to bring me back home.

But of course, I forgot to bring a picture of Ava. I have my pillow, I guess. I've been sleeping on this tattered thing for the last fourteen years, so if I need a net, I can focus on this.

Dammit.

I've got to be willing not to come back, or else I won't reach the depths I want. I bet that's how Eagle and Snake do it week in and week out. But maybe I'm being too hard on myself. Maybe as novices we each just need to make sure that we have our favorite stuffed animals in tow and our Rainbow Brite stockings way up our legs. . . . Yes. These elements must be in line before these deep excursions. If I take the proper care, at some point I'll find myself dancing underneath the ice cream cone spires at Candy Castle.

"*Oooouuuaaaack-Oouu-Oouack.*"

Ugh. My hands rush to my mouth to keep the guests from leaving before the party starts. Even though I used to do it every nervous morning before school, I still hate dry-heaving with a passion.

Hold it in. Don't complain just hold it in; it ain't that hard. Focus on the pillow—no don't. Just let her come. No sense in stopping now. Sorry, body. This is how it's gonna go. Ugh. It would be so easy though. I feel my face cringing and my lips tightening. I'm trying to hold on as long as I can. But then—

With perfect timing and saving grace, faint whistling seals my lips and the room.

I haven't heard notes this high-pitched yet serene before or that I've needed so much. There's an added element to this whistling, as if there's a subliminal layer saying, *We're all gonna be just fine.*

From the opposite corner of the room, a spinning dreidel is flung out and whirls in circles in the middle of our assembly. I know there's no wind coming into the room, but there is wind in this room, guiding the dreidel into ellipses that bob closer to and farther from all these beautiful people. The lure is made of rainbow yarn dangling from Apache wood held by the Whistler while his hand repeatedly casts out a come-hither gesture. I feel my body being picked up.

Carmela said the whistling calls the creature, but right now the air is calling me, acting like a clean shine on my mind all the while. A whirring sound comes on my left, accompanied by a pack of woozy Martians with their heads swaying and their words slurring over and over and over. The unsettling sound will stay for the rest of the evening, but thankfully will become welcome by the end.

A kaleidoscopic fractal field. Articulately infinite, colored tetrahedrons, pinwheeling in and out of each other; all of this hums over the black canvases of my lids. Opening or closing my eyes changes nothing. The song is the same. Closed feels better, though, so I clench tight, gripping my pillow, hearing and feeling metal on metal as I leave the starting gate on my way to a full-spectrum roller-coaster ride, with good and evil in the seats behind me.

For a minute, I start to go the dark road again. That vile feeling once more—the feeling of losing time and space, the feeling that I'm exploding into infinitesimal pieces rocketing to all reaches of the universe. Or is it that all complexity is careening into me? Whatever it is, it has me wishing to end it all, again. Will it be like this every time from here on out? It feels so wrong. I tell myself not to fight it too much, but my guard is way up and I don't know how much to give.

The fractals turn and flip and go berserk. Patterns grow out of each other left and right, gyrate and shift in a promenade of scarlet begetting green begetting midnight begetting orange begetting azure.

A door creaks open. Huddled together behind it are random past foes who have negatively affected my soul in one way or another. Their skin loses shape, stretches, and their faces ooze through the door opening like caricature slime of bad energy seeping in. If I let them come I'll toss my cookies before the forty-five minute mark, so I bite my pillow hard and make the door shut. Fighting myself is a dark and constant battle between sanity and revelation in which I'm not sure what side to take. They bang on the door, and I clasp my pillow tighter. In the background, sinister colors replace the tetrahedrons while I lie to myself that the affliction will be over soon. They bang and bang and yell in stupors, but somewhere I hear a placid whisper that makes the intrusion sounds less menacing. So I give, and all I can do is put full trust in her to take care of me if or when my self falls apart. I now let go of what little control I have. *Let them come.*

A white flash and I find brown straps stained with blood covering my limbs and binding me to wood. I can't say what's behind me, but in front is a chamber doused in bad hue, and repugnant shadows and trident-wielding figures line the walls as a demented pig's voice echoes through. The scent of old agonies suffocates me and makes my bowels move, before the figures crowd around the wooden slats I'm fixed to. They yank the straps until I'm not sure if the stretching sounds come from the leather or my body. And in the darkness, hideous laughter fills the chamber while they use their rusted, blunt tridents to prod me.

And across the way, tiny fallen seraphim drift and cheerful kids prance around. The children pick up objects I can't see and put them into blue satchels slung on their shoulders. A man in a cloak, carrying a small cask, crosses the chamber and settles by my side. On his head lies a broken halo with two claws protruding, and his eyes glow indigo. He hypnotizes me, drills into my soul, and forces me to look down into his cask of young, severed animal heads.

The cloaked man then slides away backwards violently whispering, as two ogres appear crouching over a bulbous cauldron. The man empties the cask into the vat as the ogres churn and sneer at me. Their bodies begin to writhe and secrete as a gigantic mouth appears and is preparing to eat me when Snake's voice breaks through the apparition. I don't know if it's the soothing quality of her singing or if it's the temporary shift of focus that has saved me, but I'm glad for whichever it was.

She sings the Shipibo way, making me wish English was as elegant of a language. Her alliterative voice pushes past the clouds in a tranquil lift, drawing us toward the vixen and vice-versa. The sinister colors fade, go back into hiding, as if they know what is coming around the corner. Articulate shapes pinwheel back, this time accompanied by shades of a circus. Then the hard-cut lines emerge, forming trees, tents, flowers, carousels, and bushes.

Something moves behind an elder tree at the center of this convoluted world. The keeper of the jungle, an elaborate, exquisite, mysterious woman: dark hair in the face, entangled with vines, braided with trees, pins of overlapping visages of jungle cats and monkeys, a colossal palette of origin emotion. Carmela and Phoenix have told me that everyone has their own version of her. For me, she appears as a jester, her face unpainted and South American, wearing a hat in arresting red and some shade of mud that almost touches black. I lock in on the ravishing brilliance in her tetrahedral eyes, before she lowers an umbrella with a hypnotizing swirl pattern and twirls it in front of me with a wink and a smile. *Why is she appearing this way? Am I in for a trick, a grand surprise?* The whirring sound comes back to consciousness again, and Snake's singing joins it this time. With beaming glances and nimble feet, the jester skips around the tree and peeks out from behind at random intervals—as if making sure I'm still paying attention.

There's an inherent sense that she knows every single detail about me. She knows about the vandalism and the kids I made cry way back when, but she also knows the good parts too, because I came from her and she's inside of me, my veins her ivy. She isn't afraid to bring out the dark sizzle, the greasy bottom of my soul, and when it's appropriate, she'll rip me apart with her divine hands. But in the end, the wounds are dressed with her overwhelming love.

Soon, the jester vixen is accompanied by a band of mute beings that emerge from the bush to populate this carnival-jungle setting. These mythical gnomes stand with candy apple cheeks, and their glutted bellies sway side to side. Over and over, they open their eyes and extend their fingers as far as they go, then close their eyes and curl their fingers into fists with accented, white knuckles. Somehow they make me think this world is real, even if it isn't. As their eyes close, I wonder why they need to blink. Why do they even walk like we do? Or have chubby fingers? They aren't subject to any rules or limits.

You guys can do whatever you want!

An abstract bop hits me solid on the head, and they answer me in telepathic ways: "This is in your mind; there are inherent limits. Now, shush, and listen."

I reengage in the adult sleepover, and Snake comes again to the forefront, escorting us and patting us on the back—each pat bringing new vividness with it—while we listen to the lullaby of the earth. Drafts of nipping air slip under my clothing, but I just want to be still, to concentrate on my breathing. I've reached a rooted peace with this position, but necessities eventually win out, and I waddle like a baby for an extra blanket. I look around, becoming vaguely aware of my friends, making out their silhouettes that seem quite content and relaxed under the effects of the soul Ex-Lax. I find my furry brown blanket and try to pull it over me, but it takes patience and skill because it's twisted on my back like a corkscrew. (How in the world does this happen? I swear this is the work of the blanket gnomes that mess with everybody's sheets. These are the secret plots we need to worry about. The truth will come to light!) I get frustrated trying to figure out the whole ordeal. I know the schematics are around here somewhere, but I can't see them among all of these layered images.

A couple more yanks free the blanket from the twist, and I come up with panther paws that go over my left shoulder and then my right in a playful game of tug-of-war. The paws bat my neck and shoulders, teasing me with claws withdrawn, and the warm fur feels sublime on my neck as my subtle chuckling elicits panther purring.

Oops. Was that out loud? Did anyone hear that?

I've at last won the panther's friendship and he comforts me now, letting my focus come back to where it should be. My stomach feels normal again, with the last of my fear floating away, and Snake's voice—which had formed a secondary cocoon around me—shrinks down into the gentle bottom layers, ending in a whispering lattice, yet still ingrained in gravitas. The song hushes down, and the whirring comes back, waiting to be covered up again. It's somewhere between

Phoenix and me, but I can't quite place its exact location. It's just there, droning at our sides, and as quickly as it reemerged it dips down to blend into the unconscious, coated by sloppy, wet sounds of organics.

THE GURGLING CHORTLE

The integral whirring is buried by the sound of someone three or four spots down from me projectile vomiting into his bowl. The retching has a powerful, guttural, gurgling quality—and the guy is doing a lot of it. With clump after clump spattering the bottom and the sides, everyone wonders how much more the bowl can take. But with ceremonial regurgitating, you don't think of gagging yourself, or wishing it would stop, or running over to take a picture. Instead, you stay back in a contemplative manner. You grasp for more, for what lies beneath. You want to understand the blackness, the negativity, the anger, or fear that's been curdling his insides for who knows how long.

A seasoned conductor of the ceremony and conscious of the health of the group, Eagle sings over the masticated food chortling, dissuading all of our minds from concentrating on the moist gargling, phlegm, and mucus, as it rises to a soggy crescendo. Though we welcome his song, it's not altogether necessary. We envision Vomitman on his palms and knees, completely under the ancient concoction, and ruminate on the hard times behind each and every upchuck. It's coming all at once in powerful, painful jolts, but with each ascension through the throat, we're at ease because we know he's begun the healing process. The walk down the hall of hell is long and devious, but at the end, around the corner, realization is dancing for him.

It's a hard process for anyone, and the older someone is the greater the odds for tragedies, heartbreaks, torments, and evils—all available to be purged. And with Vomitman in his late fifties, we feel for him and go through it with him; we want to put our arms on his shoulder and tell him it's okay, but there's the strict rule on touching each other—only if they ask first.

Through everything he expels, he brings us together. Individual purging strengthens our group, and knowing that we're all similar and need each other's help, we'll be more open to sharing our misfortunes tomorrow. I'm not sure where we are now, and I've never met most of these people before, but if I were to randomly see them on the street after this, this seeded love would emerge: "Ah, yes. I've fought with you." In this setting, this strange level of compassion is gained, this acceptance of one another's woe.

Over the next half hour, Vomitman's purging softens and slows, and I can see the fog rising from his soul. His anguish then takes a backseat to the reintroduction of the circus-jungle. The gnomes are still there. She is still there. Every hand has the hypnotic swirls now, the fat-bellied ones using the tiny paper cocktail umbrellas you'd normally find dressing tropical drinks. (It's hard to tell if the ceremony has a playful side to it, or if it's just my mind popping in to say hi every now and then.)

Vomitman settles back to his resting position, and a huge sigh flutters from his lips with the last of his dark boon. Soon, Eagle's majestic voice is all that's left, trading his singing for loud, emphatic breaths, blowing the gloom out into the night and freeing the space for good to come back in.

COMET HUGS

"Spirit of the East, we thank you for starting our journey and giving us your wisdom," Eagle says. "Spirit of the South, we call upon you now to enter our circle and teach us how to plan for the future. Once we find the areas that need work or goals we need to achieve, we must visualize the successful path, but keep in mind the need for contingency. Above all, let us learn how we will get to where we want."

I take advantage of the breather to check on Phoenix and Brown Sugar.

Are they . . . ? Yep. Still silhouettes of blanket and flesh. Good.

There's more food heaving across the room, and the whirring sound has completely evolved from an uneasy element to a comforting, almost necessary part of the evening. I hear Carmela gag cutely. Then alarming and abrasive after the lull of South's entrance, the Whistler beats on a dry and bright sounding drum. It issues percussive waves that hammer the ears and rattle all of our skulls. The beating picks up, and soon it rides at reckless speed.

Dun Dun Dun Dun Dun Dun Dun Dun.

It's almost inhuman as it is, but somehow the speed increases.

DunDunDunDunDunDunDunDunDunDunDunDunDunDun DunDunDunDunDunDun.

The drumming revs up my pimiento cheese heart until the pounding inside is so fast that I can't tell what's external and what's internal. It gets deeper under the skin, as if the intergalactic space-worms from *Tremors* spat out higher-dimensional consciousness tentacles, and instead of speeding, writhing, and quaking through the earth, they do all of it through my poor body. My organs wobble fast underneath my clattering rib cage as I feel my innards start to separate. The drumming doesn't slow down or change, but at some point, my body acclimates: the abrasiveness falls out and my heart pumps slower. The burrowing then loses aggression and dampens to a low thumping in the veins, then my skin smoothes out, the thumping turns to light buzzing, and calmness overcomes. All I feel now is astronaut-y, like there's a bounce to my soul's step. Then—

Nothing. Blank thoughts.

Still nothing.

Now a prairie. Some sort of farm. Fall maybe.

Now a dazzling wave hurtles across, turning the fields into grain, and amber follows amber in marvelous billows through cognitive space. Through time also.

I'm much older, and Ava stands beside me. It's just us—as if we're the only entities left on earth, looking over this virgin field of tranquility that beckons our wonder and surrender.

The wind wraps around us, channeling our hearts, spreading our devotion throughout all that works for us and only us. The sky turns the color I've been wanting it to, and hot orange love rains down on us from above. All we are doing—all we are doing—is being, cleansing, washing ourselves with the sun.

We're now experiencing the dream catcher side of the feather. The rolling sunlight unveils the first glimpses of the creature spirits that pour out through an atmospheric portal on the horizon. One by one, in ghostly yet crisp forms, they touch down and run like sharp echoes over the hills around us. Foxes and snakes weave in and out, jumping over and chasing each other, and an old childhood friend named Wolfe scampers with arms flailing, naked and wild by water down near the bottom of the valley. Then horses. Horses of every possible pigment gallop past Ava and me so close that I can reach out with both hands and brush their manes. The last half of the herd sweeps by my outstretched fingers, moving on to the next plain, and as they thunder on, stars, nebulas, and comets whip by all around us in an illustrious sunset wake.

The galactic mares and stallions disappear behind a small hill a few hundred feet from us, and on the left slope grain swirls back and forth from the wind that circles and caresses everything like silk. At the top stands an eagle with long legs and fleshy human features. Fertile wings spread, he leans head-on into the breeze, which ramps up on cue to send vivid eddies rushing by the contours of his body. His chest is broad and strong, accepting the majestic gales that rustle his feathers with commanding energy while his head is slightly raised and his eyes focused straight as daggers. He flaps his wings and fans them like cards again, making sure he feels every bite of air, and teaches us how truly simple it can be without blinking or bracing for any of it.

Ava and I hold hands and let the gusts batter our pupils until the dryness hurts, but from this pain, the necessity of the wind spills forth and we catch it and will take it wherever we go. Its true essence is displayed in all its catalyzing glory. It races around earth, picking up speed and surface water and smoke around us, and delivers the amalgam through Corinthian Bells, through derelict canyons, through animal lodging, through evil men's hearts, through the redwoods, and for these deeds we blow two kisses and give thanks to the Great Cloud Mover.

Now we sprint as fast as we can through amber, stretching out our arms as if trying to give the wind a hug—except no one can hug like the wind, wrapping all the way around our bodies.

We exhaust the amber and sprint through the desert, with sand prints marking our path, and feathers blow in Ava's hair while her smile might be bigger than mine. Ahead of us, it looks like the barren flat could stop short, but Eagle-man comes up quick on our right with soft, calm eyes—as if he's on his typical morning fly—and though we're at top speed, all that's left to do is sprint faster. The end of the dirt we're running on comes into view, and we put on the brakes and slide across the desert floor, uncovering a gritty symphony of our shoes scratching on rocks that rasp on the gravel that grinds on the packed layer of dirt underneath. The music's always here to be brought out, and I can't ever get enough of it.

We finally come to a stop, inches from the cliff, and the displaced air behind us catches up and rushes past, flinging limestone and dust off the monstrous edge. The white wisps of earth form curlicues off the cliff face and glide down over a pristine blue ocean beyond. Coastal air fills our mouths and lungs, and though our momentum has been stymied, our hearts gallop on, faster than the pitter-patter hooves of those galactic horses beating down on the earth like an organic drum.

Drumming on and on and on.

The Whistler's drumming comes back, and I fall back down into the circle.

How much time has passed?

Don't worry. Doesn't matter.

The drumming softens and then stops. His arm must be veining with space-worm tentacles.

"Spirit of the South, we thank you in all that you do for us," Eagle says. "Spirit of the West, please come forth and tell us of our lives. Here now is where we translate everything— what we've planned, what we've learned, what we want to fix—into living action. Here is where we put our thoughts into motion. The sun goes down in the West."

Eagle and Snake mention that it's time for personal healing. Members of the circle can now say their name as best they can and to which healer they'd like to go to for learning, listening, exploration. Some people jump at the opportunity right off the bat, but I sit back, still mesmerized by what's popping up even from underneath their announcement and not needing any more stimulation. Snake also offers a second and last time for anyone to come up and commune with the sacred brew—if a person is having trouble relinquishing control, or if they simply want to push themselves further, this is their chance. There's movement on my right; Brown Sugar is clambering over personal effects, and in the process, sends his bowl skidding across the floor. I'm not too surprised. My longtime friend has a high tolerance for this type of thing. Personally, I can feel her loosening her grip on me, telling me with her sultry, subliminal voice that the strength will soon diminish. Even so, I decide to hang back, slightly tired, slightly wired, slightly thinking it would be too much.

TEACH THAT BITCH TO DANCE

We're in a teepee now. There are no panther paws. There is no vomit. There is no pinwheeling. There is no amber swirling. There are no drums. There is no Brown Sugar. There is no Snake. There is only translation from action.

A vital fire splashes shadows on the taut animal skin above strangers that have gathered to hear others relate their integral trials. I watch a man with a half-fro and jean vest stand up, move to the edge of the blaze, and for a long beat, eye us as if it's the final time. Agitated logs send sparks across his body when he leaps over the fire, and with regretful conviction, he begins the first of three stories that embody what it is to be alive.

"I was coming down I-79 through a dim and bleak West Virginia, fifty miles or so west of the Appalachian Mountains. I was twenty-one years old, and on my way to a party in Texas, where I planned to lose my virginity to a girl who was in love with another man. It was December, just below nine degrees Fahrenheit, and the highway was camouflaged by scummy, spotted slush that blended in with the fat snow that fell down in droves. The ugly mud and oil that my worthless windshield wipers had been screeching by all day didn't help visibility, either. But even in this setting, in a Mercedes whose brakes and tires were over two decades old, I was still driving five over the limit because a girl was paying attention to me for the first time in years."

"What a selfish shit I was."

"I held the steering wheel tight as I passed tanker trucks that straddled lines all over the place, and every now and then my tires would lose the road, kicking my heart into overdrive while visions of my childhood surfaced. It was approaching midnight, and though I could barely see the road anymore, I could make out the jagged tops of the mountains looming tall in the distance.

"*Cuunk . . . Thwack.*

"*What . . . was that?*

"The speedometer needle went counterclockwise, and my gas pedal lost her oomph.

"I drifted a few feet, almost grazing the car beside me as I swerved to get back in the lane. I think someone honked at me, but by now it's tough to say. All I could think about was that I didn't want West Virginia to be the last place I saw. That, and the curves on the milk-white legs of the girl I was headed for.

"The engine fell silent as I crossed over the rumble strip and onto what I hoped was the shoulder underneath a thick, white blanket. I waited for a gap between eighteen-wheelers, got out of the car, and moved to the hood expecting to find exposed fluid and carnage, but all I saw was my breath and a normal-looking engine block. No smoke, no fluids, nothing. I went back and worked the ignition, but there was no sweet diesel purr.

"My suitcase in the back of my car had two Windbreakers. I put them on and pulled on some gloves from one of their pockets, then flipped my phone open to find the words NO SERVICE at the top of the screen. Of course not. Kiss my roaming ass.

"I was supposed to get to Louisville that night, and for a quick second, I started to wave the party goodbye, but the more I thought about hanging out with my best friend Virginity instead of the girl I'd been dreaming about, the more determined I became. So I stuck my thumb out there under massive crags and oppressive snowfall, hoping someone coming through this way was having a much better day than I.

"One car passed, window corners caked in ample slush. Another one. A tanker truck. Then a bunch passed.

"Twenty cars later, there was nothing. I was done. I was stuck out there for the night, in my car, shivering my ass to death.

"As the feeling set in, I felt my hands frantically waving above my head, pleading for someone to stop. *Please, please, please, please, do it! Stop! You! Stop! Please!*

"I sat in my car to get out of the biting wind a few times, and then went back to working my thumb when two lights veered off to the left. Finally, some great soul had stopped. But of course, as soon as the fear of freezing in my car began to vanish, it was replaced by the fear of those unfortunate scenes in Hollywood playing out in front of me on this desperate highway stretch.

"The beams were head-on and blinding, so there was no way to make anything out except it must have been a truck of some sort. I heard a door open. Then another one. They were men it looked like.

"Some definition came to their silhouettes—two burly figures in flannel shirts, jeans, work boots, and . . . kind faces. Much obliged.

"'Evenin',' the one on the right said.

"'Thanks so much for stopping. My cell's not working.'

"'Yeah, there's not much coverage around. You're lookin' twenty miles to the nearest town both ways.'

"We walked to the front of my car. 'So I had it on cruise control. Everything was fine. Then there was this loud pop or . . . whack or something. The accelerator depressed and it all went to shit.' Righty and Lefty examined the engine block. 'I tried to give it gas, but nothing happened. Car slowed to a stop and I haven't been able to start it since.'

"Lefty looked at the left side in silence while Righty checked for belts, hoses, liquid, smoke.

"'Try the ignition again.'

"'Yes, sir.' I got in and turned the key. The engine didn't sound exactly like a cat dying a slow death but it was definitely on the same forsaken alley, next to a dumpster filled with cats that got the slow part out of the way.

"Righty came around to my door. 'It's your camshaft. I have no idea what happened, but it's all messed up.' He showed me. The car was done, not drivable. Goodbye, sex.

"They offered to take me to where they were staying, a small town called Elkview, right outside of Charleston. (Don't bother searching for it. Elkview won't come up in any of your future conversations.) I left my three suitcases in my frozen, dead car and spent the fifteen-minute drive thanking them and thanking them again. I offered them money, but they refused. 'We got stranded out here a couple weeks ago,' Righty said. 'No one stopped for us and we had to stick it out the whole night. Didn't want that to happen to anyone else.'

"I learned that they were haulers, which meant that they carried people's stuff between Pennsylvania and Kentucky. They stressed they weren't movers, but haulers. If you got a lot of something you need to get somewhere—especially up and down I-79—they're your guys. I didn't ask them any more questions. I was just glad they were hauling me.

"I got my car to a Charleston auto shop the next day. The mechanic told me it would take about three weeks, but again, all I was thinking about was her. By the time the rental car place was done turning me down (some complications with my out-of-state license), it was too late for me to catch the last $650 flight to Texas, so I chose to sleep at the airport and catch the first $650 flight the next morning.

"In the end I missed the party, but I didn't miss out on getting with the girl. I did her a lot, and I did her good. I did him good, too, ruining an otherwise strong relationship. And some might say that it takes two to tango, but all that matters to me is that I was both the instigator and the one who closed the deal. A year later she still didn't have her feet on the ground, and I would still be feeling the effects of the selfish poison I injected into three lives. But not before feeling the effects of the $2,850 for the new camshaft."

The jean-vested man with a half-fro sits back down amongst the teepee crowd. A Shipibo song ends and a new one begins while a woman stands up to jump across the fire and address us. She's petite, almost fragile, but her eyes flare wide with might as she talks of tough flesh, but even tougher meat.

"With her business doing well in Japan, a determined woman from Fukuoka took a leap and came to the United States, hoping—almost knowing—she would enjoy the same success she had been accustomed to thus far. For unknown reasons, she settled on the decidedly un-Japanese state of Louisiana, where alligators are on both the menu and the mind. Chinese investors she'd worked with years earlier had told her about the benefits of eating the reptile, and every day she saw warehouse signs for alligator meat and boot stores carrying their skin. She had never eaten an alligator or seen one in person before, but after a few weeks of absorbing the local traditions and customs, she decided to start up a farm.

"Her wealth allowed her to purchase a strip of land, build proper pens, and obtain one hundred and twenty alligators. She went to hiring workers to handle farm operations while she dealt with her business back home. But though she was skilled in employee interaction, she found it hard to relate to good ol' boys, so none of them worked out for long. Maybe in a few years she'd warm up to them and be comfortable drinking Abita beer and canoeing down the Louisiana bayous, but at the time she was pretty far from it. She didn't associate with many people either, and those she did communicate with already had jobs, so she wound up having to do almost everything on her own while neglecting her affairs in Japan.

"One afternoon, she was on her front porch tallying the day's transactions, when she saw a girl not more than fifteen years old in overalls walking down the road. A closer look revealed something hoydenish about the girl that reminded her of her childhood self.

"'Hello,' the woman said. 'Little girl. Where you headed?'

"'Nowhere, ma'am. Just left the river.'

"'You just walking down the road?'

"'I don't know. I'm just bored. Been seein' if I can find any bugs to play with.'

"'Where you live?'

"'Just down over there,' the girl said, pointing up the dirt road. 'We're neighbors.'

"The woman gave a friendly smirk, thinking how much closer neighbors live in Japan.

"'Why you so bored?'

"'Got nothin' to do cuz school's out.'

"The woman considered her for a while, then stood up. 'Come. Follow me. I show you something.'

"The girl introduced herself as Natalie, and the woman from Fukuoka took her to a metal building in the back, where she told her to wait while she went to what looked like a freezer up near the house. She came back with a bucket that made Natalie's nose scrunch from the somewhat familiar but unfriendly stench, then the pair entered the building.

"It was pitch black inside and the woman said, 'Now watch,' and Natalie nodded even though she couldn't see or be seen. She heard a quick sliding sound, the bucket handle clanking, then a short silence before wet, splattering sounds a few yards away. A big whiff of stank came out of the bucket, but her concern shifted to the unseen all around her—water movement, hints of breath . . . then lawnmowers. A ton of them.

"The engine noises became guttural, violent, and close, bringing Natalie's knees to knock each other. Above them, her jaw was frightened tight, but even so, she couldn't be kept from curiosity. The woman pulled a flashlight out from her pocket and flicked it on, putting an end to Natalie's wonder.

"Seven or eight alligators were fighting, bellowing, slithering over each other as they tore apart the pile of carcasses in front of her. Almost as fast as the beam that lit them, several alligators hissed and scurried back into the unseen parts. Two of them stayed illuminated and lifted the fronts of their bodies to stargaze. Natalie shrieked and hid behind the woman, but the image was tattooed in her brain forever. The woman saw Natalie's face and decided she'd had enough. She took her outside, away from the undying noise inside the building, so she could calm down and they could talk.

"'I know you scared, but alligators no attack humans,' the woman from Fukuoka said. 'They scared of us. Beside, walkway very safe, fence strong.' Natalie could only breathe, still shocked from seeing a kind of carnage she never had before. 'I need someone to feed them every day.'

"No words came out still.

"'I need help when I leave town,' the woman tried again. 'You say you bored. You help me or what?'

"'I— I don't—'

"'It's simple. They feed once a day. Four pens each hold thirty alligator. I teach rest of duties tomorrow.'

"Natalie stood there pondering the job. She wondered if she could go through with it even once more, let alone for the two and half months of summer still to go.

"That night, she discussed the opportunity with her parents over Tuesday meatloaf. Her dad said it'd be good to learn how to handle money and responsibility but questioned her mental strength, and all her mom could do was worry, as Natalie knew she would. After they deliberated over and over, Natalie was the one that came up with the idea to take the job on a trial basis.

"The woman was flustered by the request, but her options were few and too far between, so she agreed and in thirty minutes told Natalie what she needed to know about the farm and the alligators. She said they were usually solitary creatures in the wild, but when they were crowded in pens, the effect was a heightened sensitivity to light and sound. So she always kept them in total darkness.

"After a full day of wringing the sweat out of her shirt and impressing the woman with her ability to handle the chores given, she found herself with a bucket over the freezer, digging around in the meat. She wasn't grossed out by the dark pink mush and stink, but again and again she was haunted by flashes of the snarling death-rollers. And with the bucket now full of nutria, beef, chicken, and fish, Natalie stood with red hands and an anxious heart, hoping to skip the next step but still gain the courage that only comes after."

"Natalie stopped outside of the entrance, took her shoes off, and set the bucket down. She took her hands to her pants, but there was no dry place to wipe them. At this point, all she could do was play the woman's pointers over in her head: "'Best to be silent or they get stressed. Some sleep near fence. Throw meat far as possible.'

"Inside, she stopped on the artificially heated concrete, and tried to quiet her breathing. The dry walkway she stood on split the four pens and was the high point of the warehouse. From there, the concrete ramped down to the leathery bodies that were more often than not huddled in the shallow waters beginning halfway down either side.

"Sneaking past her parents' bedroom was nothing compared to this, Natalie thought. She tested the fencing that lined her path—just glorified chicken wire, with several bent-in areas about as large as an alligator's head. Natalie put away as many of her doubts as she could, sucked it up, and started the first of what she hoped to be many successful strolls through the reptiles.

"The tricky part wasn't sneaking down the walkway to the pens, it would be coming back after the food sloppin'. Natalie worked it out in her head and then chose to feed the furthest enclosures first, but the infernal hissing from isolated spots stopped her thought process.

"She gulped.

"The sound of reptilian skin sliding on concrete made her hair stand on end.

"*Natalie. You're holding dead animals. They're gonna smell.*

"Natalie's hand trembled on the bucket handle, the alligators undoubtedly getting riled up. Instinct took over, and she used her heavin' arms to spastically throw the entire bucket of meat into the first pen on the right. Her first throw left something to be desired, with half of the meat pile plopping a foot or two from the fence. The chorus of lawn-mowers rose, and with no Japanese woman to hide behind, she turned on a dime and ran out of the shed.

"She was disappointed in herself. She couldn't think clearly inside the building, overwhelmed by the hidden aggression. She felt like the job could be too much for her and told her boss so. The woman thought it was nonsense, but she would help finish the day's feed, and Natalie was to come back in the morning.

"That night, Natalie replayed her mistakes and developed a new plan. She still didn't know how to conquer her fear, though. She couldn't conjure that hypothetical scenario. But she did feel something she had been longing for: excitement.

"The next day Natalie showed up to work feeling proud of her persistence and thinking the woman from Fukuoka would be surprised. The woman gave her no such satisfaction, but did give her a list.

"'Here. You help with these, too.'

"After she was put in her place and her tasks done, she prepared four heaping buckets and set two outside the building before hustling the other two all the way to the far pens. Her plan so far intact, she brought the first bucket back, gave it a good sling, and heard the ever-more-familiar splat of meat on concrete. She went for the other bucket, aimed at the opposite pen and heaved. This time she heard the meat land on the living.

"The hissing began.

"A few alligators snorted. Her body was fixed. She tried to shut them out, but images ran through her head of cleaved animals blanketing the alligators, their gaping jaws dripping with the desire for flesh. There was no way she could use her flashlight. She was in it now.

"*Calm down*, Natalie thought, *just use what's in front of you.* She reached for the fence and snuck her fingers up to the railing. She walked slow and silent, running her hand along the top, hoping no alligators would rise up and chomp on her fingers. On her left, there was ample movement—heavy tails flapping back and forth, crazed slapping sounds. She tried not to panic, her silence her protection. She felt the fence rattle behind her. There was growling and slithering on her right, then a snap so loud she swore it was right at her ear. Struggling to stay in control of her bladder, she moved faster into a light jog that caused a bucket to clank off her leg then off the fence, and in no time at all, there came bedlam from all sides. She yelped. She covered her mouth. She hurried on, and finally seeing the crack of faint light from the bottom of the entrance door, she abandoned the jog for a sprint down the remaining stretch, her buckets banging off the sides of her legs. She reached the door and burst forth from the shed with a cloud of dirt and relief, her buckets sent to the air as she fell to her knees.

"Her boss came out of the back door of her house to see about the commotion and saw Natalie panting and two buckets rolling to stops on the ground beside her.

"'Why so much noise, crazy girl?'

"'I did it,' Natalie said, panting. 'I did it. I fed them.'

"The boss lady went over to help the girl up. She pointed to the full buckets on the side of the shed entrance. 'Why those buckets have meat still?'

"Natalie blushed briefly, but recapped how she almost got through with her plan before she had to run out again. Her boss was annoyed but saw progress. Once the girl gained more confidence, there was a chance she could be a good helper.

"The swell of summer came on, marked by off-the-gauge temperatures. At the apex, the mirages were oily and thick, and with the humidity coming off the gulf, Natalie's shirts wouldn't last long. The grime and salt built up quickly, and she would end up buying new clothes every other week. It was hard work for a fifteen-year-old girl, but by summer's end she had gained the respect of the woman from Fukuoka, and the two developed good rapport. Natalie continued to work even after school started up again, and although she never got the new fencing she would go on to ask for, the woman did agree to add more wooden reinforcements.

"'Okay, okay. We make fence better for poor little, helpless girl. But it come out your pay.'

"Natalie didn't make as much money as she had thought she would that summer, but over her time at the farm, she acquired something more valuable, something she would use for the rest of her days.

"She saw what she needed to in her rural life, and when she got older, she moved to a bigger town, becoming a musician once there. Natalie hadn't grown out of her stature, but she acquired a captivating voice. She joined up with a group that saw this too, and when they wrote songs, they would make her parts the loudest. Audience members at their shows would see this fragile woman and think nothing of her. But during the harmonies, she took herself back to the farm, and used what was way down in her gut—weathered with the spoils of those violent pens—to belt and howl and surprise every ear. She was the one that fed the crowd, that they depended on.

"She learned to control her fear. It was an insolent bitch at the start, but in time, became a partner in everything she did. She was able to direct it, to dance with it, and they were beautiful together."

The woman takes her seat with the rest of us in the teepee, and soon all that's left is the fire crackling. From the back, a shrouded man moves to the hearth. He takes off his hood, but no face emerges, just billowing smoke and black hair.

Without speaking, he jumps into the fire, disappearing as if sucked into a vacuum. The flames shoot and flee from themselves as if trying to expel Smokeface, and then, somehow, he communicates to us through blazing, telepathic sparks:

"In the fire, I am creature,

Outside, I am man,

But the fire stays lit forever inside me,

Out of the fire, into the pan."

The fire throws ragged scarves of heat in odd directions and spits out not verse or word but man of smoke and shroud. He stands motionless, then stretches an arm out toward the hearth, his hand blossoms open, and at once every flame funnels into his palm.

Smokeface then draws the hand back under his robe, leaving the teepee fireless and dark.

The canvas disappears, and I'm back in the world of Eagle and Snake. The moods of the room are again whisked away by the ceremony leaders through accented outward breaths.

Sssseeuu . . . Sssseeuu . . .

"Spirit of the West, we thank you," Eagle says. "Spirit of the North, we welcome your guidance and hindsight. We started our long journeys in the East. Are we satisfied with the outcomes we've faced? Are we on the right paths? What will we decide to change for the better? We look to you for the evaluation of our lives."

I completely forgot that the cardinal directions are leading us through the ceremony. The West seemed like it went on for hours. I can't believe we're only three-quarters through. And though I'm out of it enough to realize how tired and hungry I am, I don't want this night to end.

DREAMS AND SQUALOR

Eagle asks one of our fellow journeymen to take us along with him, on the heels of his instrument. With his breath comes melody, and I'm wrapped tight, bundled right, in a blanket of tribal peace. Cylinders of auburn and autumn orange radiate from my pupils, as I'm struck with awe and stuck in wonder, gazing up through the color structures. I'm not sure if it's a drone or a double, but I'm certain the magic from this flute is most rapturous, more than any other. This hymn through wind should never end; in fact, it won't, for I'll take it wherever I go and act as its continuous bellow—all I need to remember my ancestors from long ago.

Wind. Pfff.

That guy just doesn't know when to stop.

With immaculate music conjuring it all, I'm in a car traveling toward mountains on a long desert haul. I hold a frayed book and look through clear spots of a muddy car window, where every now and then I see remnants of the life I've known. Speeding from sunrise, the morning gales brush the dirt off, revealing the landscape of my sparkling dreams and my persistent squalor. And my uncle's coal-black mustache sticks out among the sand and hay as he keeps pace alongside us, making dust clouds with the four-wheeler he was killed on by a dirt rocket rider jumping a dune he couldn't see the other side of.

Behind his helmet and sunglasses, his thick whiskers, I can't make out his face too well, but he's looking straight ahead to the mountains we're closing in on. He raises his arm and sticks out a finger, pointing to the peaks, at what looks to be our Mexican ancestors' faces. They're out floating in the blue behind them, as big as the mountains themselves, and their eyes are fixed on the acreage that fans out beneath, that stretches fast and disappears as it curves. This is the second time in a week I've seen them, and they're telling me they have only one message: there's lots of work to be done.

We keep driving toward them while I read a book that I know I've seen before but can't quite place. This trip feels like a long lullaby, but it's not trying to make you sleep, it's designed to keep you up for days.

I turn a page of the book, then glance up to see the car setting has been traded for my old room—the first place where my imagination was free to run wild. I'm nine years old now, crossing multiple storylines and universes, throwing Legos, Micro Machines, Ninja Turtles, Transformers, all into the same fantasy. There weren't a lot of villains in the bins, but there was usually a string fastened to a high point and heroes on the floor at the other end. And there was more than likely a boiling hot moat that everyone had to get across, with some making it and an equal number falling short and melting. I held quite a few action figure funerals in my childhood, preferring to steer away from fairytale endings.

My parents knew I spent a lot of time with my toys, so they made sure I spent time with books, too. They kept a quiet— *Ah. That was the frayed book I had in the desert.* It focused on our solar system, and at the end there were pages and pages of hypothetical aliens or creatures that could inhabit each planet, like ice monsters on Neptune, fire demons on Venus, and other strange life-forms on Pluto. I remember I loved the possibility of it all, the vision. I thought how great it was that authors, illustrators, scientists, and others worked together to come up with aliens that were true to the climate of their respective planets. Sprawled out on the hardwoods, I read the book over and over, because back then I was sure I was going to be a science man.

I was sure because Daddy was a science man. In some ways, he still is. He saw the affinity in me at an early age and made sure to keep that bug in my ear, giving me countless math and science books, and we would talk about them and what they meant. We were closer during that time; it felt like there were no taboo topics.

It's what set me on my path to the cubicles all those years ago. But with everything I liked about math and science, I didn't love how they were implemented in school. And though I could find enough enthusiasm for people to believe me when I told them I wanted to be an engineer, it took me quite a while to realize I never felt it in my heart. At the time, it was a solid plan that made my dad proud, and back then, that was enough. But a lot of time and effort later (almost all of it), I found my thought processes stifled. There was no openness or freedom. I missed being able to create alternate worlds and make up fantastical situations and see how to get through them.

I feel it in my old room now, but I know it's not permanent. None of this is. I know the presence of my parents looking over me now as I flip through the solar system is not real. It will all fade away soon. But it feels so good, so right. They're caring for me and I'm not shutting them out. I miss this closeness with them, the ability to simply communicate.

Man.

When did that go away? I want them to hold me again. I want to replace our long-lasting drift with renewed mutual interest. Mostly, I want my father to be able to look into my eyes again and be proud of who I am.

There's no point. They won't understand.

I've been living this double life for so long. I can't take it anymore.

No, it's just easier this way. Think of what would happen if you did.

It's not that I can't think of anything to talk about, it's that I'm afraid to.

No, I'm not. Am I?

I'm . . . Has it really been me? Has it really been my fault? No. I don't know. Maybe it is. No, of course it is. Of course it is. I've been so selfish.

But it was their money. Their time. With their ideals, how would they not be disappointed, even disown me?

Reaching around my sleeping bag, sifting through all the emotional bricks that are hitting me, I go for an extra shirt to wipe my face dry.

I cherish my parents as much as I did when I was reading in my room all those years ago. I wanted them to be there back then, to feel safe, and now I've pushed them away. They have no idea who I am.

I can't keep on doing this. How do I go to them as myself? They already lost half their faith in me when I quit; they only care about me making money. They wouldn't listen, would they?

THE CRASH DOWN

My tetrahedral vixen wraps her arms around me and takes me elsewhere.

That's enough for now, she says. She's given me enough heartache and work to do with my parents for one go-round and knows when she needs to stop. *Take me, my jungle sweetheart.*

When I first started this journey, I was overwhelmed by the all-encompassing affection she wielded. She helped me reach extraordinary heights, from some of which I tumbled down; but before the splat of meat on concrete, her tranquilizing hands have clipped in to save me just so I could experience the freefall and imminent death along the way.

She tells me there's only one more thing to do: a last visit to Ava—my soul mate, one of those entities to be born and destroyed with out there in the fields of perpetual ether. In our terrestrial world, only a glance from her would be needed to make me forget that I'm a breathing organism, her existence a beacon of such intensity it somehow outweighs the baffling thought that we could be together. But it shouldn't be baffling, because though our skin is different, the truth is in our cores; in our hearts there's a tiny shard on which we can gaze at each other's reflection.

Powerful as that truth can seem, so too can timing be a diabolical bitch. Because of her long, consecutive run in the dating world and my lack thereof when we met, Ava wanted to grow and to explore on her own—a need that I admired and encouraged at the beginning—and she wanted me to venture out, too, to learn from other relationships that would hopefully come my way.

However, that sentiment or anything else couldn't stop us from communicating every day or planning entire weekends together. Liberties were consistently taken, lines were blurred, and every month that Ava said she could not be with me yet, we grew closer. It was irresistible. I would go on to tell Ava that she was the only person I would drop everything for, and in turn, she said I was the only one that had ever made her believe in marriage.

It soon became that every day I hoped there would be a knock on my door, and I would go to answer only to catch her already crossing my threshold. The day's dazzling yellow would be cast acute on her heels in mid-crow-hop just before she uppercutted the air and yelped in her spunky voice, "I'm ready!" And on that day, the light behind her could have been sucked up into the sky, and the entire outside world could have gone to blackness, and the temperature could have plunged down toward absolute zero from the obliteration of the sun by some unseen cyclonic calamity jettisoned from beyond the far reaches of the Deep Field, and I wouldn't have cared or even known that anything was amiss because her love paired with mine would be all I would perceive and need to remain alive.

But that day never came.

I told myself to hang on, just hang on for a few more months. How could I stop when I've never been affected on that level before? Unfortunately, seriousness and everything that comes with it entered the picture, and after nearly suffocating the butterfly in my hands, the only move left was to loosen my grip. But the slack I gave was too much and came at the time she needed me most. It was such a short span, but I wasn't there for her and the damage was done.

Still, there is a faint yipping in my subconscious as possibly there is in hers—a notion that time, like some sort of twisted, veteran prankster, has a plan, and you just have to ride it out and accept the less than ideal situations because they can only be temporary in the end. So I keep going. I have to keep treating Ava like the force she is. What else can I do? Persistence is the only way she'll remain in my world to any degree, and if my role is only meant to be a supportive rock for her, then that's the one I have to take.

But right now, the jungle jester unveils a foxtail hanging from Ava; it sways in a herky-jerky fashion as she shimmies her backside over the threshold of some house. I watch her hair gleam with curls—the hair I've felt working between my fingers so many times before. And she wears the sunglasses I always want her to take off so that I can see the sun sparkle in her irises. On one sun-iris-sparkle day, we ate opposite ends of a message carrying stem, finishing in a meeting of the lips, a kiss of ecstasy through which came the knowledge of each other's soul. That afternoon, life was supreme. Since then, she's given me a steady supply of transcendental fixes for long enough that I'll never flatline, because I know there's always a possibility that life can be that grand, and is.

She's in my arms again, and we lie on a couch in my house. In the past, I've joked how I was slightly afraid of our love ever being fully realized—in all my projections, a part of me was afraid the happiness would fill me up at raging speed until my heart exploded. But stepping back from it all, every moment can be like this. It's not just those like I had at the campfire, it's every moment. My job isn't to selfishly control them and keep them inside all to myself so they never leave, it's to feel the come, feel the go. They always come. They always go. I should just let that happen.

So as Ava gets up from the couch and moves toward the door, I only watch her in her rapturous glow. I'm not getting up. I'm letting her flood of ardor and passion crash over me with perfect crest and perfect trough.

And somewhere down beneath all my memories and soliloquies, a small, desolate part of me feels like this is the last time I'll truly be with her. My old self would fight it, soak it in, and try to imprint her meteoritic presence in the ageless thoughts that have kept me up in Neverland skies. But now I see that a wave is never a wave forever. It's only serene because it crashes down, because it fades out, because it makes way for another.

We admire them, day after day. We're on the same beach, looking over the same bountiful water. But to feel the power of the ocean, we have to get wet. We have to go to that perfect point near the shore, that sweet spot, to experience the whitecaps in all their beauty, up close and immersible, and know that the crash down only means there's another crest on its way—another crest unlike any this shore has ever seen.

So there Ava is, making her way out into the future. She crosses the threshold of my house, her exit bathed in perfect, bittersweet light. And with the sun we both worship touching down on her angelic hair, she looks over her shoulder at me and blows a painful kiss goodbye.

CHATTY CATHYS

Eagle rings his bell, signaling the end of this leg of the trip. "Fear not," he says, "for the experience is far from over." He goes to turn the lights on as Snake tells us we're free to talk among ourselves, to share, listen, or both. Up to this point, not a word has been said between the circle members, aside from Snake and Eagle, so like a chorus of fifth graders asked to share their summer vacations, everyone turns into a Chatty Cathy relaying their revelations:

"How'd she look to you?"

"I spoke to my grandmother."

"Did you see music?"

"I wanted to run away."

"I saw my old ranch."

"How was this compared to last time?"

"I saw myself being born."

"How in the world is your bowl not full?"

While my other friends and I ramble on, Brown Sugar is silent, entranced with the floor, his head moving drunkenly from side to side while his hand covers his mouth. He meets my eyes, but sort of looks past them, like there's another driver at the wheel. He motions with the hand at his mouth, making sure I know he took a second cup.

"Oh, I saw you," I say with a wink. It's rough on him, but he manages to answer.

"I'm definitely still in the . . . thick of it," he says, gagging.

A few seconds later, he empties out into his bowl, and as before, only now with lights on his convulsing body, I watch and nod my head. Attaboy, Brown Sugar.

As he vomits, Phoenix, Carmela, and I share what we learned and saw: the exhilarating bliss, the blanket of affection, the global view. The brutal dissolution of everything we hold true, too. We all feel like we saw death together—the same death I experienced the week before, they're describing to a tee.

"It was like all corners converged into me," Phoenix says. "A shrinking triangle of nothingness. Collapsing and merging. Like every single image occurred with or . . . cut through all the others."

"I thought the same thing!" Carmela adds. "Except I felt like I was falling down a never-ending well, trying to stop myself. I felt like I died beside you guys tonight. Aw, I don't want you guys to die. Give me hugs!"

"Yes!" I say. "I mean . . . I don't want you guys to die either." We hug each other like we haven't touched anyone for years.

Every minute of the next twenty feels better than the last. There's a comfort in knowing there's so many more ravishing experiences to embark on or create, unpleasant aspects to turn marvelous, and we get to enjoy that side by side. I look at my friends and I want to put gold stars all over their faces. *Dammit, thanks for being here. Good job!* I would have never thought being given so much work could feel so fulfilling. And I get to share it with my dear friends? *What? We're not even at the best part yet?* I could get used to these penultimate times.

We go outside to stretch our limbs and whims, and to look over this Lone Star land. It's restless and tireless underneath the satellite that's used to being the loudest player of the night, but tonight the lead roles are played by the stars. Every single one is so bright, so there. We can almost see the plasma burning. They're all up there, laughing among themselves like it's some sort of inside joke:

"Yeah, you forgot how massively everlasting our radiance is, didn't you?" one of them says. "Even when we're dark and rubble, we're workin' the night shift for you, beyond the grave."

"I tell ya, we get no respect," another one says.

We're all bathed in survival right now, we pulsars of love, wired to the deck and letting the juice all play out. Our surroundings sit primed. Every foot of this ranch weaves and breathes its cipher out into the night for the eddies to carry through, whispering over faraway ground the blankets of ideas old and new. The extrapolation of creation is so vivid—so livid—on this supernova highway we're all bustling on. Every particle around us is buzzing, humming with activity, saying, "We're all here for you; we're all meant to be, too." Holy shit, there's so much going on, so much to take in. And everybody can be plugged in to sense that all matter is living, through thick and thin, through us and them. It's a simple and pure cure to the havoc and chaos, seeming like loss but not, for we see and hear that "each piece is here, right where and when it needs to be."

It's going on right now. And right now, also. I'll always be immersed in it, whether I'm taking the light to it or not.

Eagle brings out his bell again and has everyone reconvene in the circle. "Well, I hope everyone got some good work done," he says. "Thank you for being a part of this special evening. I can't tell you how happy I am that we all made it through. Make sure to get rest, because tomorrow morning is when we go outward, where we'll share our experiences with the group. Feel free to continue chatting, but do so quietly so others can sleep if they want to."

Ummmmm . . . what?

Turning to Carmela: "We uh . . . we . . . I can haz dinner, tonight?" I ask.

Carmela and Phoenix look at each other, as if they'd been hiding that information from me the whole time. Phoenix raises his dirty blond eyebrows and tries to smile while Carmela says, "Sorry. We're not gonna eat until morning."

On most nights I'd be mad. But had I known, I probably would have been weighed down with worry about the awful headaches that come when I don't eat—a probable barrier for the soul magic. I'm thankful they didn't tell me.

We haven't eaten in fourteen hours, but it's mostly from all the visuals that punched me in the breadbasket, the concentrated living, that my body and head are like a pile of dead meat that's been baking in the sun for too long. It's all been worth it, though. I'm never excited to speak in public, but I'm exuberant about tomorrow. I can't wait to hear of everyone's trials, everyone's champion runs. And with taxed eyes, I look around at all my fellow beings tucking into their sleeping bags and can only think, *What a most eclectic adult sleepover this is.*

It's about 1:30 a.m. on earth, and the crazy creature celebration orgy is about to burst out in a frenzy of frolicking shadows all across the early morning sky. It's time for us to trade one dream world for another.

Good night, moon. Good night, my red creature shadows bouncing in the sky.

INTEGRATION I

Clanging pots put an end to my dreamless sleep. My body's a little sore from lying on hardwoods all night, but the gears are lubed, ready for action, ready for implementation. I feel so light, and it's not just from lack of food.

I'm more than glad everyone cleaned out their purging bowls last night—regret, suffering, and loss probably don't smell good the next morning. What does smell good is the coffee and tea brewing that have everyone stirring, enabling me to see faces for real for the first time. The evening gifts and morning drinks have Carmela, Brown Sugar, and Phoenix beaming, as am I.

Eagle passes by with his bell, the bell, his jingling silencing and stopping all, even Brown Sugar's constant flibbertigibbeting with his curlicue hair. Eagle takes his spot alongside Snake to lets us know how it'll go. "It's time for the first step of integration," he says. "You may share your intentions, your experiences, your findings. Be mindful of the time limit, and respect the drum mallet privileges. Also, it's important to remember that this room, including the people in it, is pretty much the safest place you can be for sharing. There is no judgment or fear in this space."

As the mallet is passed, so too is knowledge from pinwheel land: Some speak of past hardships that resurfaced or that they didn't even know were there. Some speak of seeing their constant struggle with their place in the world. Some speak of puking like never before, but seeing nothing in their bowl. Some have near breakdowns just communicating their transformations. Many speak of relationships with parents or family that they need to repair. Others speak of not getting to revelation land and being fine with it, because while the vixen plays a crucial part, the rest of the ceremony is just as important, even if you don't embark.

Brown Sugar expresses emotions that I've never seen from him, even after knowing him for fifteen years and living with him for four. And after showing us his underbelly, leaving the circle tingling, he passes the mallet to me. I thank the leaders for the music, and I thank my friends and everyone else for being here. Then I get to the heart:

"She reminded me that the one thing we can all see, the one thing that supports us no matter who we are, is the same for a general in Korea, a doctor in Finland, a soccer mom in suburbia, a baby in Brazil. We can look up to the heavens for answers, but right now—at this current juncture—finding common ground between all of us is paramount. And it's as simple as looking down at what held the feet of those before us and what will hold whatever's after us, the bridge between our past and future. The core, her heartbeat, is a whirring ball of fire so dense, so energized with blazing love that we can feel it up on the surface. We can share this innate power with each other and give everyone the great earth hugs they deserve, because she can't do it without us.

"She also showed me that there are thousands of different plants sprouting from her abundant soil. Each plant of hers has a different way of growing, hooking, climbing, reaching for sunlight, but in the end they all get theirs just the same.

"I've only begun to comprehend her words, but they already bring me such peace."

My friends and I agree that sharing with our walls down is the best part of the ceremony— the most engaging three-minute speeches we've ever heard. You can really get to know another when they're completely honest and unafraid. By the end of the morning, the various stories and the people who tell them begin to dissolve into each other. With our skeletons and treasures displayed, we each go through what the entire circle does. They say if you take her right—sticking to the diet, respecting her, abstaining—that she will forever be with you. Well, if I were to be honest, I've only felt a few fleeting moments, and even those are suspect, but I can say with strong conviction that the first part of integration changed my life in sixty minutes.

After the mallet makes its way through the circle, Eagle reminds us that this was the easy part. The second step is our reintegration with the world—much harder, but nonetheless we each have new knowledge to put to use in our individual lives. However long it stays, however it gets expressed, I'm excited to go back into the world with a renewed spirit.

And with that, Eagle lets Snake make the announcement I've been antsy in my pantsy for the entire morning: "I hear breakfast is ready. Let's eat."

Eating has never been so relevant. All the food is spread out on two tables like edible virgins ready to be deflowered, ready to give away their sweet sustenance in my mouth. I load my plate with all the sexy fruit, scantily clad vegetables, devilish quiche, and voluptuous bread, but before I head for my seat, I think twice about indulging in my desires so I can grab more immediately. I know I can go back for seconds later, but that makes too much sense right now, and my stomach is such a barren bitch that I'm surprised it hasn't started eating itself.

Walking to the tables, I look into everyone's eyes and nod.

Wait a minute.

I rarely look at strangers' eyes. I'm the short, shy guy. Honest. But man, right now I'm throwing one of my biggest weaknesses to the wind, and it feels right. It feels easy. It feels like I've always been doing this. I'm even making eye contact with Vomitman, and I go to sit next to him—another thing I don't normally do. I give a hearty handshake to the man who threw up for a solid half hour a few feet away from me last night. He clutches my hand in that way that kind of hurts but makes you feel special, makes you feel like you're worth a damn. We talk like we've known each other for years.

After hearing someone lose their insides all night, social interaction becomes simple. There's nothing else to do but be myself. I strip it all down, but the simplicity's always been there. After we died next to each other, we've found ourselves alive together. And it's good. Damn good.

We can pal around right off the bat!

But not before eating breakfast. Nothing comes before this breakfast. Nothing.

Every bite of fruit, vegetable, and quiche is an angel's orgasm of immaculate nectar—the booty of my experience. I've always found the expression "I'm hungry enough to eat a horse" to be completely ludicrous. Until now. I could at least eat the ribs, legs, and—

Sorry, that's terrible. I love horses. I love horses. My beautiful, galactic mares. My comet bringers.

After eating only about a hoof, I make sure to get the food off of my shirt and down that, too. We clean up, everyone packs, my friends and I say bye to a few people, and finally thank Eagle and Snake again and again. Another great thing about integration is that you realize Eagle's a normal man and Snake's a normal woman. Sure, they've gone through a lot of mental training to get here, and their psyches need to be strong to deal with the burdens, but they still walk like we do. They're in the same world we are.

Whoever it is, we've all gotta go through the Labyrinth just the same. We gotta get deep in there and hear each step echo in all directions. And just as we think we know the way to the center, with the answer so clear in sight, we get spat out and splattered against the outer walls. But at the far reaches, we all keep on the expedition, listening to the insides of our veins. We follow the ivy. We go even though we slowly realize we have to traverse every inch of the spiral to dance with our Minotaurs: our ancestors, our orgasms, our murderers, our eternity, our revenge, our plight, our enlightenment, our God, but most importantly ourselves. We all have our different colored threads to get back out, too. It's just that Eagle and Snake have been to this Labyrinth before. They've gone to a different center each time, but they know how to use the thread. Even if we've been to the Labyrinth before, we sometimes need them to be Ariadne. But once outside, we reach a different state, and to know that your mind will be different when it faces the next challenge is sometimes the only comfort needed.

The gift of wisdom comes to you when you have walked enough pathways and found enough dead ends to truly know the forest. In the discovery and rediscovery of every inch of ground comes the knowledge that nothing ever remains the same.

We make it back to Carmela's house and hole ourselves up for the next day and a half, creating the good buffer we need between vixen land and the trenches fat with mud. It seems like every hour her parents go out to get more food, bringing us more of the finest fruits and pastries in all the land. *Yesssss, my precious . . . .*

We've never eaten so much before. Our gullets are infinite and unquenchable. Bring me more of the food. All of it!

In between belly feedings, we go through what happened the night before, sifting and rooting through each other's visions, finding striking similarities. We share for hours and even Phoenix stands up to act out some of the physical parts of his evening. I'm glad because it's ingraining the ceremony even more. There's no noise in the background. No chatter. Just communicating, resonating . . . and the eating.

I'm rubbing my belly when there's an itch on my ankle that I go down to satisfy, but forgetting about the spider bite temporarily, my nails scratch in pus. I stop to look at the bite, and it's gotten worse. I show Carmela, and she tells me what spiders represent: fate, female energy, creativity, starting a project, becoming pregnant, infinity, trickery. I feel pregnant with food right now, so maybe there's something to it. Carmela insists she rubs aloe on it, but I don't want it to heal. It feels like a risk I should take (famous last words).

The next morning, Carmela says she dreamt of a gigantic demon in the room where we all crashed, so she had to go sleep with her mom. Another ceremony was held after ours in the same place and she felt like she was there, waking up to the presence at around the same time that we all went under the night before. Phoenix and I couldn't imagine doing that two nights in a row, or even twice in the same year. We already have so much treasuring and simmering to do, on top of all the other work given.

Luna comes back from running more errands for us, and we sit at her mammoth dining table while she tells us how the second and third ceremonies can be much different. She says the first is to warm up to the concoction and once you're used to the feeling you can go deeper. The one that hit her the hardest was her third, but the first she did with her daughter. Carmela nods and gives a slow grin. I tell Luna I'm jealous that they could even do it together because there's no way my parents would consider participating. She asks me why, and I say they're set in their ways, content with their lives. But I do want to know how to tell them of the ceremony, to which she replies, "You know who to ask."

Carmela and her mom invite Brown Sugar, Phoenix, and me to their land that used to be a Native American trading post, which I haven't been to in years. It's oddly in the middle of the city, and plenty of businessmen have tried to buy and develop it, but as long as it's in her family, Luna will never sell. Tucked between two major streets, it offers a few rustic shelters, building-tall trees, and unabated green runs. Aside from infrequent car noises, the city really dissolves away, fostering good reflection.

I arrive early because I want to take the space in alone for a while, to sit on a rock shelf and let my mind go. I look up in the trees, and far on the left I see the black box, the owl's nest that Luna spoke about. And I nod and smile.

Thanks, my guardian night bird.

My body feels weightless. Any leaf or stone or chair I look at is new, brimming with possibility, but I am also grateful for what it is. This is the most at peace I've ever been in my life. I can never go back to my old ways of sitting in idle as the world flies by. I'll dig and dig and dig inside the moment, and find how fertile even the toughest soil can be. And I know where I have to start first. What an end to such a crazy week.

PART V: EARTH SURGE

TOMMY AND THE CHAMELEON STEW

While out at the ranch and in the land of pinwheels, Eagle briefly told us what we might have in store, and I couldn't help but picture him in an infant throng of other harbingers of new pillars emerging from the horizon and coming fast for a landscape already booked or not. Among them, representatives hold accounts of past prophecies as possible time guides at their side, which always makes me question would particular works of the world have come to be if old seers had not issued forth their divinations? But just the same, Eagle's oracles of choice have an immediate quality to them and are drawn from the sacred books of Chilam Balam (jaguar priest), where cyclical forecasts for the next three *katuns*[1] can be read.

In katun 2-Ahau, from 2012 to 2032: "For half the katun

---

[1] *katun:* a period of time spanning 7,200 days (approximately 19¾ years), used in the Mayan calendar.

there will be bread; for half the katun there will be water. It is the word of God. For half of it there will be a temple for the rulers. It is the end of the word of God."

In katun 13-Ahau, from 2032 to 2052: "There is the universal judgment of our Lord God. Blood shall descend from the tree and stone. Heaven and earth shall burn."

Finally, in katun 11-Ahau, from 2052 to 2072: "There cometh a white circle in the sky, the fair-skinned boy from heaven, the white wooden standard that shall descend from heaven. A quarter of a league, a league away, it approaches. You shall see the dawn of a new day, you shall see the mutbird. . . . The heavenly fan, the heavenly wreath and the heavenly bouquet shall descend." This katun has been interpreted by Kenneth Johnson as "the Renewal of the World."

No matter the weight given to this aged set of texts, some believe there is a framework solidifying as we speak, one that offers volatile years ahead, but one that comes with advancement in all fields and ends in a coming together of the minds, an outcome that we've been on the path to since the dawn of humanity.

Deep in the jungle, Little Tommy the ape cleans his friend's back and eats flies as he picks them off. With a stomach full of fungus, the flies buzzing with high-pitched voices send him backwards to the turf. His friend's back loses shape and oozes out into a caress. For a second, he's drawn to the new movement, but fear enters as it spreads toward his chest. Things are getting too crazy for Little Tommy, his world is changing too fast around him. All he wants now is to stand on solid ground, but his canopy is closing in.

"I'm getting outta here" are the first words he says ever.

On his way out of the jungle, he notices how ridiculous his hands and feet look, but they don't hold a candle to his weird, protruding tallywhacker. Away from the canopy, underneath a speeding and breathing sky, the brush grapples with each other, and the water slides by like caricature animation, as a bewildered Tommy rubs his eyes.

Maybe, I'm the one that's crazy, Tommy thinks.

Visions of novelty hurtle through his reality. He's thinking. He's thinking about his thinking—his Kubrickian monolith.

And hundreds of millions of years ago, a white, thread-like organism grew in the water. It may have helped plants take a foothold on land or may have itself been the dry life starter; but since then, this latticed-root type structure has taken hold of the dirt and made networks that seed and sprout like the Internet all over the earth. These networks have immersed themselves in their surroundings, acquired traits, aura, and history. Meteorotic spores aside, they've been helping life along, from water to land, Little Tommy to man, giving us knowledge along this mystery. The microscopic complex has taken Universal shape, colonizing the soil, mirroring the pattern of the brains that presently colonize this world. And now they fruit like penises and atomic bombs, but they could help in bringing back the calm, ending this unfortunate moratorium and being catalysts for the times to come.

It'll be quite the millennium for mycelium, a true cause for celebration.

And Little Tommy knows it, cuz he's dancing now, and dancing mad. He's shaking it because he knows he will be free—all of our children will be one day—free from the rigid structures of old. He'll be a part of a generation who will reap

205

the rewards of educational, psychological, medical, and technological miracles that are almost through the assembly line.

Little Tommy will see rampant traffic fade away into the cornfield dimension. Facts carved into stone will cease to be not because they'll be worn or outdated but because the stone itself will sublimate. His teachers won't need to strike through lesson plans, because they'll already be in the trash, traded out for the new paradigm: learn while you do and do while you learn. Instead of being in school for seven hours a day—good training for the cubical life—Little Tommy will access streamlined, complimentary online courses that cover the gamut of most sectors worldwide. Through easy-to-use, open-source software, his friends will be able to investigate any problem they want, and may even find better solutions than their elders because their minds will operate on a wider plain. And with 3-D printers on the desk of every son and daughter, our children will have a blast adding to the global movement of manufacturing ingenuity, not for monetary gain, but for being creators, seeing their educational pursuits bloom in front of their eyes.

As Little Tommy grows up to be Big Tommy, cultures will become subcultures, and vice-versa, across the seesaw board. Movements will gain steam in the U.S. culminating in FDA approval for therapeutic uses of MDMA by 2021. Ph.D.-led university research programs already under way will result in legal use of natural plants and fungi for treating PTSD, addiction, end-of-life depression, the autism spectrum, anxiety, cluster headaches, and cubical slavery. Big Tommy and his friends will trade abusive environments and the desire for the instant fix for self-discovery and the co-evolution of language and consciousness. They'll all go on the inward journey, like

Terence McKenna's apes, but one day it'll be accessed freely by the organic being. They'll utilize the dimethyltryptamine which is present in our bodies but currently resides on Schedule I lists for the U.S. and the UN. And as public happiness waxes, abundant stigmas will wane. Alcohol and tobacco use will take a dive, too, impeding the growth of funeral mounds containing the millions fallen at the hands of legal drinking and smoking.

But just as in our minds, there's evil blanketing Tommy's world. He'll have to be ever-cognizant and grounded as the number of black shamans—who will prey on the weak, fragile, and unready—will rise in parallel with commodity corruption, impurity in edible and human form, and the chase for superficial acceptance, the fitting in with the trends of this world. And people will be outraged! But the pockets of evil and what they brew are a small price to pay if there's a chance for some of the world's richest and most powerful to take what so many have taken before to witness more connection, more compassion, Jeffrey on Jupiter, and to be nudged into world problem-solving through teamwork across every ocean.

But what if that doesn't happen? Big Tommy's not worried, for the sacred, the ceremonial, the ritual preparation will ride the lightning and prevail. "Signals from the planet just feel right," he'll say, absorbing messages that have grown and solidified over billions of years inside the earth's crust, and translating them into meaning inside himself in a moment of elegance and bliss.

After catching a glimpse of what remains untapped in this world, he'll throw a party to celebrate, but people will tell him, "The human body isn't meant to eat four cartons of birthday cake ice cream and go skydiving."

"Then what is it meant for?" he'll say. "Where is it written? Where is the sacred parchment? Is it five, ten, fifteen items long? And it's constant until the end of time?"

They'll run off, thinking he's crazy, holding on to their old ideologies that stamp out the fires of potential.

"Species don't adapt and survive without radical change!" Tommy will yell. "We don't need these old grains."

Big Tommy will be confident in his longevity because he'll have a specific, genome-guided diet and health program that spars with early death. If a lung fails, he'll have extra in his fridge, or he'll wait for a few hours while slice after slice of a new one is printed in his home office. If disease gets creative, he can too, and counteract the dysfunction inside him with enzymes from a species that's completed the process of de-extinction. He could even witness the end of aging altogether when medicine finds a way to cure ahead of the curve—a fulfilled prediction of people like Aubrey de Grey—that will keep Tommy eating his ice cream into his hundreds, four hundreds, or even thousands.

"You have to work longer then, invest smarter," his dad would say.

"If it's just a few more years, I agree, Dad, I do. But what if Dr. de Grey and others push us way out to two hundred and two? If I'm thirty-three with a Ph.D., and I don't stop working until I'm a hundred and fifty . . . carry the two, divide by servitude, that's a hundred and seventeen years, Pops. Are people going to spend that many years in a cube? Well, we do it for forty years now, so maybe. But that's terrible, Dad. Isn't that a little crazy?"

The people in Tommy's world will take their staplers, diplomas, and daily reminders saying WITH ENOUGH COFFEE

ANYTHING IS POSSIBLE, and run out into sweet freedom air, yelling, "You can't have my soul for eighty more years, Norman! I can be a butterfly too!"

But then what would they do? Once all the pandemonium calms down, then . . . then the real magic will happen. People won't just quit, no, they'll quit and they'll learn. They'll teach themselves to order chop suey in Cantonese or to woo lasses with tenor sax skills. It'll be commonplace to have the entire alphabet after our names, representing unprecedented numbers of job and industry changes. After five years of donning scrubs, Big Tommy will live in Ukraine to study folk dancing, then spend five years in a particle colliding lab, then he'll go to Africa to compete in ostrich racing. He'll realize he's got a whole mess of time on his hands to get his shuttle license, to carve figurines out of topaz, and to write the genomes of new species. He'll find complimentary patterns and construct buildings by song, use cuttlefish skin to design clothes, and grow organic laser shows with stoplight loosejaws.

But that's not all.

What if Mozart lived for four hundred years? He'd finish the *Requiem Mass*, deliver a crescendo of concertos, and experiment with early techno before trading his pen and piano for a chisel and anvil, fulfilling his blacksmith dream that had always been pushed to the background. With Tommy by his side, he'd hammer on weapons with a sort of clean ringing metalworking shops have never heard. Then one snowy night, on his 398th birthday, a sweaty and pale Mozart would slow his steel pounding while his two pet wolves reared and bayed in the firelight. He would barely be able to raise the hammer anymore, as Falco's "Rock Me Amadeus" neared its end in 6-D sound, playing from his deep bass speakers that

209

run on hydrogen. At the climax his hammer would drop, his body would follow, and nothing would be left except the echo of the last clang off the most sovereign and pristine sword never fully forged.

Longer life span will change everything.

But at a most important juncture along Big Tommy's path, he'll see a vast crevasse, Chilam Balam style. On one side, the ticker watchers will stand, with their turtlenecks, high-and-tights, pinstriped suits, cigars and brandy, and their massages and printing presses. On the other side, the love coalition will stand, with their colorful socks, long locks, hemp clothing, joints and tea, and their massages and printing presses.

In the middle will lie a raging river of the building blocks of tomorrow, and on both sides, people will scale down their respective cliff face with backpacks of dynamite sticks to accelerate the erosion. But hopefully Tommy will see Peter Diamandis's "three billion minds" rise up from the river, one right after another, drenched with answers, seizing dynamite and laboring to repair the bridges that have been broken for so long.

Or he won't.

But the lines are dissolving. We're mixing fast, we ingredients in this cosmic inferno. The dial's turned up, we're reaching a real nice stew, and the bubbles of universe wide epiphany are making their way to the surface. No matter how we got here, no matter what kind of garden or process line we came from, we're healthy with each other at the right proportions. Dinner's hot and ready, so come hungry, get full. Because life tastes good, and it's good for you, so have a second bowl.

But there will come a time when we will all get eaten, too. Life springs up out of dead animals and plants—isn't that the universal rule? Stars die, stars are born: conception by supernova. Get your interstellar fireworks right here! Stagnation, you better move over.

We're unearthing the secrets of planet-building material, helping us escape red giant status, and the reactor's humming and glowing ethereal, injected with the DMT lattice. We're set on our course, getting closer to critically massive proportions, and we're barreling down this supernova highway, with momentum lubing the pistons. We're about to open up to full throttle—now using megalithic conversion—because this planet is nuclear, baby, and we're already far from notion.

EMBRACE THE MAELSTROM

As Tommy grips it 'n' rides it, every day he'll watch a new proof arise that will transform the way he and his peers think. Tomorrow, global geoengineering will buy humanity the time to get to a place where interplanetary Internet will be useful. The day after, AI robots will help us in every hour of our schedules, and reports will come in fast that some have carried out the decision to execute us. Not much later, the world will turn upside down when the link is made between the first group of hive-mind volunteers, testing the very concept of our individuality. He'll watch.

Tommy will remember that in 1903 two brothers rode the sky in a powered craft with popsicle-stick wings, and a surprise airstrike from Japan caused clouds of black cauliflower to plume from sinking battleships in 1941. He will remember that only eighteen years later, the Soviet Union launched a spacecraft that impacted the surface of the moon, and in

2013, Voyager 1 became subject to the conditions beyond Neptune.

Big Tommy will watch as the 100 Year Starship, a project whose mission is to make human interstellar travel a reality by 2112, will prod experts into studying sea slug photosynthesis, suspended animation, and every element necessary to overcome the obstacles that space possesses. Breakthroughs will arise in nuclear fission, self-renewing machines, and human bone strength, not only benefiting the project but also the quality of beings here on earth. He'll watch. The applications that spawn will be under the public eye because we'll have all helped them appear, but further down the road, we'll discover sources of immense energy, how to warp space-time, and new means of propulsion, which if given any thought at all, could be used toward darker ends. He'll watch as any outlier that's connected at any time will see the seeds of evil laid out in the open, ripe for the picking. And at some point, the volley of unchecked power will find one tormented soul—one soul brought to drastic measures—and there his finger will hover, inches above a button to blot out the sun.

We've hit the ramp fast. Our parents and past hold on for their dear lives, not ready to go. They choke our wrists red, but in this instant, we suspend physical feelings. Check back in a few moments . . . maybe.

No sounds of road or rubber anymore. No shimmying chassis. All we cling to are the seats we sit on, worn with the imprints of those before us. As we hit the apex, there's absolute chaos. There are ghosts, bad dreams, and murderous beings. There's a confused, young girl across the aisle looking up at her mom, but all she can do is hold her child and brace her for what's to come. Some of us strangle on to hope with every limb while the crazies run to the head of the bus to take their front row seats to destiny. There's a few of us staying calm, somehow knowing it will be all right. With a confident nod, they attempt to reassure us: "We'll land on the other side, and it'll be better than we've ever dreamed." The low hangers fall in line like usual. Others think it's a good theory, but need more convincing.

And then there are those of us who can't help but think, *This big, beautiful bitch wasn't made to be airborne.*

Looking through the glass, a hundred yards below us lie piles of broken tube televisions, half-erased chalkboards, junked telephone booths, beat-up baby grands, and combustion engines for days. We'll either overcome this gap or fall just short of it and plummet to our final resting place—down there in the land of the almost and the never again.

We can almost make out the other side. The driver leans forward, his toes white in his shoes, giving her all the futile gas she can take. There's no telling what will happen at touchdown, but it'll be violent. It'll take everything she has to correct herself. But for now, the driver's done what he can do, and all that's left for this bus is momentum.

All we have left is momentum.

We're experiencing survival convergence. We're studying and transferring the structures and rules of our ecological world, priming us to be computerized beings that farm manufacturing facilities using biocomputers that give birth to themselves. And the mimics have begun to mimic the mimicking of each other—and exponentially, too. The homogeneous pile will feed and feed on itself, adding to the avalanche of information that's already careening down the mountain. The fleet of data will be so much to process, the now will eliminate our drive to be prescient. And we'll all surrender to this massive flow in unison—the focal mega-shift to the present.

Terence McKenna thought nature preferred this change over habit, this trending toward more complex states: "There really is a purpose to the universe: Its purpose is this state of hyper-complexification in which all of its points become related to each other, become—what mathematicians call—cotangent. It gives the universe the feeling of being imbued by a caring presence."

Billions of years ago, Tommy the Amoeba and all the other unicellular organisms showed us the way. They collected, developed communication, and formed the higher functioning multicellular organisms. It felt good making something bigger. And every day we acquire new tools to be responsible for our own evolution—and evolution loves company.

In this way, any iteration of points is as important as the next. So we need shamans to teach us how to feel the wind like eagles and ground vibrations like snakes. We need mathematicians to fill pages with equations to get to one number. We need physicists to propel us into realms we've never seen, but have always been in. We need spiritual lightworkers with their interdimensional DNA activation and $400 orgone pyramids. We need doctors and researchers to optimize the meat inside our skin sacks and keep pushing our expiration dates further out there. We need peacekeepers and activists to advance relationships and be lobbyists for love. We need the autistic and schizophrenic. We need Facebook and the future websites that replace it. We need international conglomerates. We need meth heads. We need crippled people. We need girls at festivals asking for money to staple on their faces. We need skateboarding CEOs. We need evangelical atheists. We need racist philanthropists. We need mosquitoes (I know, I'm sorry). We need orgasms. We need you. We need me. We need every piece to inform the next, for this is the way we will reach our great reward, whatever that may be.

We're taught from a young age to shoot for the stars, and we've achieved so much in this space-age realm, yet only a sliver of the universe has been revealed. Ninety-five percent of the cosmos still sits in wait, but we're slowly upgrading our minds to ease and tap into this hidden force. And maybe we only need to map out a portion to find approximations to make a complete celestial blueprint. Maybe we'll see similarities between the cosmos and us, and vice-versa, in a neverending loop of awesomeness and fine honey mustard. We'll learn to wield that which is dark to merge dreams with reality and to live in a constant state of awe under our bodacious canopy. With satellites and telescopes twirling around in gravitational pulls uncovering space, chips implanted in our DNA, plants and fungi, or—better yet—completely opened minds reaping the rewards of 4.5 billion years of planetary evolution, in this culmination of life as we know it, everything will draw inward, for the universe will be inside our minds.

In the future we won't have to shoot for the stars. The stars will shoot for us.

As mentioned, we've begun a starship project to get us to the Alpha Centauri system within one hundred years. And many of us are already living across the galaxy or up in the heavens, which is understandable—at times, it's difficult to live in this multidimensional land of proliferating craziness, powder kegs, and exponential fragility, but we should not be afraid to embrace it. On this rumbling terrain, where fractal behavior literally keeps us alive, acceptance of the seemingly chaotic flow of scenarios will ease the mind. The more we embrace the entropy, the more it will start to make sense. The great concrescence of technology, religion, society, spirituality, nature, and science is quickly coming upon us. We'll all be drenched in it at the center of the maelstrom. We'll get to these higher orders of complexity and organization, the next steps of evolution, and become masters of the universe, able to bask in the brilliance of galactic beauty and paradise. But there's one piece being overlooked.

It's already here. . . .

We don't need to get there. It's always been here. And it always will be.

There is an escalation within all things now. The twenty-first century has been placed at a vital crossroads, perhaps the most important in our history, and the convergence of industry and the communication between all different life-forms in parallel will be what guide our planet. The answers we seek are already woven into whatever is in our hands and whoever stands beside us. And the interaction that draws them out waits as a creative fuse, ready to spark volatile change, ready to be a small, necessary element in a chain reaction that has continuously complexified since the origins of earth. Keeping this in mind, only in the present moment does creativity lie, and from the experiences herein, one of the ways I've found to be at the center of creation is to simply give thanks. But a better way is to give thanks with you.

SCARECROWS DON'T SWIM

A short jog away from the early spring picnic is the slope of grass where Magnus grabbed bunches of dirt and rode the earth. While Ava's trinket-laden fingers lay out her pickle salt and discs of fried cheese, I share the camping-to-ceremony week in a flurry that ends with one of those heart-galloping embraces guaranteed to stay with me until my last days. Tears slip down her face and genuine words follow, but when it's quiet again, there's still a marked difference between the feelings I glean from her and the ones that dwell inside me. She's entrenched in my psyche, maybe more than before, but like after an alarm interrupting an ambrosial dream, I have to snap out of it and painstakingly remind myself that she didn't live through what I did. It's a repetitious and arduous task to keep myself in check when I'm around her, but I try regardless.

From time to time, Ava and I still manage to find those glitter-filled and gold-saturated moments together, but it's not like it was. It never will be, I guess. Ava's boat raised its sails and caught the jet stream I fought so stubbornly to keep her out of. But what has stayed with me, what she has left behind, is the phrase I used to cringe at, but now embrace every day of my life: "Hey, scarecrow, don't worry. The only constant in life is change."

With additional years under my belt (and sometimes muffin-topping over it), I can't help but think she's the original fountainhead for my passion and consistency. She showed me how to be the juices of life, harness them inside the veins until they bulge from the love all around this great rock and the power in our hearts. Because of that, her force will always shine through my blood. And wherever I am, knowing that she's somewhere out there—beyond complacency, beyond the rules, experimenting, reveling in the new—is all I need to feel alive. Somewhere in the temporal mix of the winter firelight and the wake of galactic mares, I've realized that all she was I now carry with me; because she helped cultivate my life, I can leave her soil. She's set me on this rewarding and crazy course, and that's how solace is reached. After all that's transpired, I wouldn't change a thing.

Six months later, an outside force puts a timer on the prolonged and unspoken impasse between me and my parents: at long last, the hour of the piper is at hand and opening up to them is the only legal tender. This isn't just any conversation to be had on a whim, this is the one that really tests the nerves, the one where I show them everything in the mud.

I give them a week's heads-up, and I try to convey without actually saying it that it's going to be a big one—a dialogue where spoiled repression will come to light, for good or for bad. But the week plays out like time travel, and before I know it I find the back of my heel rubbing nervously on their couch in anticipation of Dad coming home.

My mom has of course put out her spread of crackers, dipping oil, prosciutto, and assorted nuts for me. She asks if she can get me any water or Sprite or beer. "That's okay, Mom. I can get it myself." She tries me again—am I sure she can't get me anything? "Mom, really. I'm fine. Thank you." And I say all of it with immediate regret for the unintentional coldness I answer her with.

The rest of the time, I don't do much. I just sit there, staring out the back windows into a yard where I've done so many things I've never told either of them. Mom turns on the TV—*War Horse* is halfway through; she keeps it muted.

We sit in the fat, relaxed silence that's become the norm over the recent years but today is laced up tight with awkward oddity. Every few minutes, Mom reaches for crackers and I check the time.

I don't stop checking, but she eventually stops reaching.

Silence.

"I had a dream last night that really—" Mom starts, but stops to look at the ceiling, gathering her words. "You were just a child. We were in a metal building, or at least the walls were metal. And I had you on my lap, and I was very apprehensive. And you just kind of sat there. Because of course, you didn't know what was going on. I didn't know what was going on. But all the people around us were total strangers. And a lot of them—the women—were wearing these cassocks and bandanas."

"Cassocks? What are those?"

221

"They're just kind of—I guess you would say long, billowy robes. And even the men were dressed the same way. And strange dialect; I couldn't figure it out. But the children had on these really heavy coats. But you didn't have a heavy coat. I didn't have a heavy coat. And the last thing I remember was this person yelling, 'Get down. Get down.'"

She reaches for a cracker, chews it methodically, and looks over her yard through the back windows, at the yellow grass in waning light.

"How'd you feel after you woke up?"

"Just . . . not right. I looked around and wondered if I was really there or not."

We sit in another stretch of silence as I stare down at my hands. Looking back up, I catch the confusion and uneasiness that have taken over her eyes.

I chug water with nervous speed and relieve myself countless times over the next couple of hours. I try not to plan the speech out, but I do anyway. And finally, after dry heaving in the bathroom thinking of what comes next, I exit to the sight of my dad walking through the front door with fresh bread and folded newspapers under his arm.

There's no pride in it, but with the rub so close, I suck down two bottles of beer and more than a splash of whiskey to calm the nerves. I tell them the first half of my speech, the safer half: my optimistic views of the changing world, and their opposition to or denial of it. Dad disagrees like I knew he would, but does so with a calmness I didn't expect.

"It has nothing to do with religion or any transcendental values," he says. "I'm talking about human nature. These marvelous Greeks, over two thousand years ago, stressed the principle of 'first know thyself.' Mankind has never learned that lesson. Despite all the progressive issues you talk about, people keep oppressing and imposing their views on each other, we continue to have wars. You can call it what you want, original sin, whatever. Mankind has never overcome his flaws.

"I'm talking about staying within the boundaries right here, within our experience. These technological improvements you speak of haven't improved man one damn bit."

"I can't imagine what it was like growing up when you did," I say. "And I know it's hard to find hope among global bloodshed, I'll give you that one. But what's the one thing on everyone's mind? What's revolutionized everything we do, no matter if it's in a boardroom, coffee shop, science conference, or festival? A man-made invention that connects everyone. Because of that, I can't help but have hope that the 'every man for himself' way is losing its hold. Humanity will come to stand side by side, to look out over our creations, because we need each other. We all feel it deep down: the desire to be loved. And technology is helping us."

My father brings up Sisyphus and his boulder, and goes back to the well with "history repeats itself." But as I continue my rebuttal, I realize this is the first time in years I haven't been hesitant to speak my mind. More importantly—and surprisingly—it's become an invested dialogue. Ah, I remember this feeling, and this time sitting in a lap isn't required.

What generous spoils have come for me this day!

Having lost my train of thought, or maybe because in something my dad said I feel like we've found a common ground, I decide to go full-bore, to spike the needle.

"I'm here because I haven't felt the love we used to have since I was young. You guys don't know who I am anymore.

223

I should be able to tell you guys everything, to be open and honest. But I now know a lot of it is my fault, and this time the soul-sucking job can't be the excuse."

As the sun goes down, my chest remains bare, and I tell them everything: the power in my lawn chair, the bouquet diet, Vomitman and Jeffrey. I worry that it's a little too much too fast, but when it's been bottled up for so long, it just explodes all over you. And after I've lubricated my insides, even developed an exit strategy, the backlash never comes.

"When your dad and I heard you were working Sundays, and when you were even working in the hotel room when we went to visit your cousin after his food poisoning bout, that's when we knew something would happen," Mom says. "We just waited around until it did. Then we stepped back. You have to have room to grow, to be validated. Everything's been dictated and planned for you, up until you quit your job. Questions arise. Why am I doing this? Is it making me better? Pushed over the edge you had to find your own way, you had to explore. We're glad you're able to be honest now. You're young, and there's so much going on—maybe too much. We love you and we always will."

I don't know what to say. I was expecting a fight. I repeat the key topics to make sure they're listening, but no one storms out, they only ask questions, more engaged than ever. Engineer or not, I'm still the boy they care for. And at long last, a wave of relaxation hits me when I realize the second step of my integration has come to completion.

I can now admit that the biggest obstacle to my progress was myself. Faced with the terrifying possibility of change, I willingly became the bottleneck. I was so preoccupied with knowing the exact outcome of the talk with my parents that it blinded me, stifling my action. But the reality is that factors had already changed. The flux happens whether I address it or not.

So instead of fighting the flow, I now let the waters come, and embrace the maelstrom. And as nightfall rolls in, no matter what happens next, my parents and I are left with what's within the boundaries right here, within our experience: the love between us.

REFERENCES

49, 197   Jamie Sams and David Carson. *Medicine Cards* (Bear and Company, Santa Fe, 1988).

121   Steve Pinker. "Steven Pinker: The Surprising Decline in Violence." Available at http://www.ted.com/talks/steven_pinker_on_the_myth _of_violence.html.

203   Ralph L. Roys. *The Book of Chilam Balam of Chumayel* (Carnegie Institution, Washington, D.C., 1933).

204   Kenneth Johnson. *The Mayan Prophecies: The Renewal of the World 2012–2072* (Llwellyn Publications, St. Paul, 1997).

205   "Fungi Helped Plants Move to Land," *Astrobiology Magazine.* Available at http://www.astrobio.net/pressrelease/3671/fungi-helped-plants-move-to-land.

206   *MDMA: Keynote at Psychedelic Science Conference 2013.*
Available at http://www.maps.org/conference/3-day-conference/.

207   Terence McKenna. *Food of the Gods: The Search for the Original Tree of Knowledge—A Radical History of Plants, Drugs, and Human Evolution* (Bantam Press, New York, 1993).

208   Aubrey de Grey. *Ending Aging: The Rejuvenation Breakthroughs That Could Reverse Human Aging in Our Lifetime* (St. Martin's Press, New York, 2007).

210   Peter H, Diamandis and Steven Kotler. *Abundance: The Future Is Better Than You Think* (Free Press, New York, 2012).

213, 216 *100 Year Starship.* Available at http://100yss.org.

215   Terence McKenna. "Terrence McKenna: The Strange Attractor" (1998). Available at http://www.youtube.com/watch?v=Cget6JxSpfQ.

ACKNOWLEDGEMENTS

My parents for understanding, sticking it out. Adam for a long, amazing friendship, and for putting up with all of my stupid shit. Sam for exploring long digressions and progression. Matt "the fucking doctor" for inventing the Internet. Andrea, my constant sun worshipper, for opening me up. Javier for "listen to your heart." Croft for his passion for the shots, and his DP hands. Chris C. for his tutelage, and Chris U. for his tootelage. Monica and her mom for being such generous angels. Alison for constant strength, support, and mac 'n' cheese. Mark for purchasing dinosaurs recently. Andrew for his steady nicknames and being my rock. Dani for being the best friend anyone could have. Trey for being a bro in LA, and our future projects. Cole for all bifurcation and pontification needs. Thrashley for getting brutal with me. Neda, my down-ass chick, for living with a hermit. Brian for always asking how my day was. Morgan for showing me what art can do, where it can go. Claire for being my partner in crime for so long. Spring Chicken. Chase and Kana for advice. Lance and Bryn for reading and being in my life constantly, even when they're not. Andy and Vance for thongs and taints, brothers from another mother. Steve for metal and Adult Swim. Donny for coming to Coachella. TED for positive possibility. The SSS crew for the early sausage years. The PSU crew for warming me through the frozen tundra. The TBC crew for some outrageous times that I wouldn't trade for anything. The EEA crew for lunch conversations. All the Purple Warriors for Thursday heaven and so much more. The Wolves for taking me under their paws. Earth for you. And ultimately David K. Fried for patience with the pile.

ABOUT THE AUTHOR

Armand Daigle received undergraduate degrees in Nuclear Engineering and Mechanical Engineering from The Pennsylvania State University. After being an MEP consulting engineer for five years, he now works as a development producer for Lobo Sucio Creative. *Thank Earth You* is his first book. He lives in Austin, TX.

8840392R00135

Made in the USA
San Bernardino, CA
25 February 2014